THE GREAT BRITISH GHOST HUNT

Books by Hans Holzer

GHOST HUNTER
GHOSTS I'VE MET
YANKEE GHOSTS
GHOSTS OF THE GOLDEN WEST
LIFE AFTER DEATH
THE PROPHETS SPEAK
THE AQUARIAN AGE
THE PHANTOMS OF DIXIE
THE POWER OF HYPNOSIS
HAUNTED HOLLYWOOD

HANS HOLZER

The Great British GHOST Hunt

The Bobbs-Merrill Company, Inc.
Indianapolis/New York

In memory of the victims of
Culloden, Glencoe, and Flodden

CONTENTS

THE GREAT BRITISH GHOST HUNT

INTRODUCTION

After ten months of intensive preparation, I was finally on my way to the Great British Ghost Hunt. The young lady from British Overseas Airways Corporation had assured me that the press was notified, both here and in Britain; the captain of my flight had been alerted; the hostesses were aware of my impending arrival; and no stone had been left unturned, no matter how old, to flush out any ghosts I might have missed in my preparations. I was to go on an evening flight, using one of British Airways' new VC–10s for the first time. "Do you realize that the length of your plane is the same as that of nine limousines parked nose-to-tail?" Miss Mann, the publicist, said when I came to pick up my ticket, looking at me with a challenge in her eyes. I assured her that one limousine would be quite sufficient to get me to the airport. She then handed me a fact sheet containing such useful information as, "Your VC–10 is as tall as a three-story house, and a game of cricket could be played on each wing." I found it more fascinating that the plane used four Rolls-Royce engines, as I had always wanted to ride around the world in a Rolls-Royce. Immediately, I felt luxurious all over.

At the airport, everything went smoothly. I was examined, as is everyone, for any hidden arsenals I might carry and then ushered into a softly lit half-filled VIP lounge where I could await the call. The bar at the rear of the large room was well stocked—in fact, if it had been any better stocked it would have been necessary to put the bottles on the floor. Several of the passengers who had evidently arrived a little earlier than I were already slightly off the ground. I checked my main luggage, taking only the motion-picture camera, my still camera, and my tape recorder with me, along with some correspondence which I always take on long flights. Suddenly a terrible thought struck me: I had forgotten about Elizabeth's gift. Elizabeth is Elizabeth Byrd, whom you will meet later on; she is a friend and fellow author in Edinburgh, Scotland, and she had suggested that I bring her a bottle of Scotch. I felt a little foolish importing Scotch into Scotland, but a wish is a wish, so I quickly raced back through customs, picked up a large bottle at the duty free counter, and resumed my wait.

Finally my plane was called, and as the big bird took off from Kennedy, I settled back into my seat and decided to attend to my correspondence. The plans for my ten-day stay in Britain had all been worked out to the last detail, so I could relax. Of course I had been to

Britain many times before, gathering material for this book. But this time I would do some ghost-hunting in areas I had not yet visited. In a manner of speaking, then, this was the culmination of years of research, and I was very grateful to the hard-working people at the British Tourist Authority for getting me a decent room to stay in, for in London getting into a hotel is always a problem.

Of course I wasn't going to stay in London and do my ghost-hunting from the window. British European Airways would fly me to the provinces, and friends with cars would get me where I had to go in places where airplanes couldn't.

I was so involved in my correspondence that I had almost forgotten I was on an airplane, when all of a sudden I heard a popping sound. I recalled how the friendly publicist had mentioned proudly that ear-popping was no longer a problem as far as the VC–10 was concerned, since the plane rose to its cruising level very gradually. When I turned around I realized that the popping sound had come not from my ears but from the bottle of champagne a lovely blond hostess had just opened. They were starting the dinner service, and apparently were going to wet our whistles with some high-class champagne. A lifelong vegetarian, I had requested a vegetarian meal. It turned out to be as good as anything I could have had in a first-class French restaurant. I decided that my expedition was going to be successful since it had started off in such a satisfactory way. As soon as the hostess had taken away the dishes, I returned to my correspondence.

Somehow she caught sight of my name on one of

the letters, and after some hesitation, which I ascribed to her British temperament, she came over and asked whether I might by chance be *the* Hans Holzer. I assured her that I was, there being, at least to my knowledge, no other, but if there were, he would probably not be so interesting as I. Having established my identity, I learned to my delight that she had read several of my books, and was, in fact, quite psychic herself. Since things had become a little quieter in the plane now, I invited her to occupy the empty seat next to mine and to tell me all about it.

Miss Wilson (not her real name) told me that her mother had been psychic too, and she felt she had inherited this gift. Her father, on the other hand, had always scoffed at it, as men are wont to do, but she was quite sure that it was real, and she wasn't in the least afraid of it.

"I know that it is from God," she explained, "and I use it frequently, when all else fails. For example, one night I was in New York, and the weather was bad. Somehow I got delayed in returning to my flight out at the airport, and I began to worry that I might miss it. All of a sudden, I had a flash, telling me, 'Your flight will take off two hours late,' and it sort of calmed me. I didn't even care that we arrived back at the airport half an hour after the supposed takeoff."

"Was the flight two hours late?" I asked.

"It was. On another occasion—I think it was last December—I had a peculiar dream. In fact, I woke up from it in the middle of the night, because it had been so vivid. I saw my cousin George, whom I hadn't seen in years, standing by my bedside looking very, very pale, and there was a gash on his forehead. Before I could question him, he faded away. But I had the distinct impression that he wanted to say good-bye and that something terrible had happened to him. Now George and I had been quite close, even though I hadn't seen him for some time and hadn't even heard from him for at least a year. The dream disturbed me greatly, so I wrote to my aunt in Berkshire, telling her about the dream and asking her how George was. A special delivery letter crossed in the mails with mine: George had been killed in a highway accident while motoring to London, on the exact night I had had my dream."

I nodded and explained that clairvoyant dreams such as hers were not uncommon.

When Miss Wilson learned why I was going to Britain she offered to come with me on one of my ghost hunts. The idea naturally appealed to me, so I encouraged her to call. Unfortunately, her schedule must have intervened. But if she should read this account of our pleasant conversation, I hope she will accept my invitation to whatever ghost hunt I might be going on next.

One of the more common misconceptions among Americans is that Britain is full of ghosts, that the British love dearly to tell ghost stories, and that every castle has at least one resident ghost. On the other hand, America has comparatively few ghosts, and new houses never have any. All of this is simply not true. But one thing is true about British ghosts: they are colorful. Britain has had a complicated and frequently violent history. She is a comparatively small country, with people living close together, so ghosts and hauntings very much reflect local conditions. Since the various parts of the British Isles differ greatly in the character and personality of their people, the ghosts remaining in these parts of Britain are also quite varied, and what may be of great concern to ghosts in, say, the New Forest in England's south may have absolutely no meaning a hundred miles away, and the world of Scottish specters is totally different from the "surviving emotional memories" of an unfortunate spirit caught between two stages of existence in, say, East Anglia.

My first attempt to have a go at British ghosts was in 1964, prior to my writing *Ghosts I've Met*. I'd heard reports of a haunting at Windsor Castle and requested permission to visit for that purpose. The librarian, Robert Mackworth-Young, assured me that there was nothing to those reports. The closest I came to nailing down any ghostly accounts about Windsor Castle was a story relating to King George III. It appears that shortly after the king's death a guard was passing by on the terrace outside the royal apartments and glanced up at the windows. To his surprise he saw the figure of the king behind one of them. Naturally, he gave the customary salute and the figure gave the customary response.

Generally, I was made welcome by the English people whenever I came to call for ghostly reasons, but when it came to official residences and palaces, things moved a bit more slowly. Despite some well-supported accounts of hauntings at Sandringham, one of the royal residences, I was unable to gain permission to visit, even when the queen was away. I managed to go through the Tower of London, and if there are any resident ghosts left, they must by now be sick of the tourists. Likewise, Hampton Court is allegedly haunted, but an investigation there is almost impossible because of the tourists and because the official attitude does not favor a serious psychic investigation.

Nevertheless, ghosts are serious business in Britain. According to the Associated Press, Lieutenant Colonel Algernon Bonham-Carter went to court because he had ghosts on the first floor of his house. The colonel argued that the presence of the specters was diminishing property values, and he therefore requested a cut in his real estate tax. The court agreed with him and reduced his taxes by 10 percent.

Britain offers not only new and hitherto undiscovered ghostly manifestations in many of her historical houses, but an overall renaissance in occult matters, ranging from hauntings to psychic readers, most of them far superior to the American variety, and from Celtic temples still filled with the original magic to *Wicca* or witchcraft, being practiced by a number of covens from the top of Scotland to Land's End in the south. If ever any place deserved the name Magic Isles, it is Britain.

There is something in the atmosphere of England that makes one do things he wouldn't do in any other country. Somehow the ever-present feeling of great antiquity mingles with the legendary mystique of a place where history was made, or the ancient gods were worshipped, to produce an electrified aura which gets to you the minute you set foot on British soil. If you are, in addition, inclined to delve into the occult, you will perceive and sense many things that may only brush lightly by ordinary visitors. Thus, it wasn't at all surprising to me that shortly after my arrival in London in April, 1973, I received a call from my old friend Alex Sanders, High Priest of a Wicca coven, inviting me to a very special ritual in honor of May Eve. Visions of Walpurgis Night appeared before my inner eye: how nice it would be to ride up to the British equivalent of Faust's *Blocksberg*, meet all the pretty witches, stay clear of the devil, and have a ball. Of course, nothing of the sort was promised me; just the contrary, as I knew very well that Alex took his Pagan rituals seriously, since I had been present at many of them in the past. But I accepted the invitation with pleasure, inquiring only where the ritual was to take place. I knew that Alex and his wife Maxine, who acts as High Priestess, had a flat near Notting Hill Gate, just twenty minutes from my hotel, the Cadogan. But apparently this ritual was going to be held in the country, and at considerable distance from London.

Now Alex can be very exact, but he can also be very vague, especially when he gives directions. "Take the train from Victoria Station," he instructed me. "Go to Berwick, and then look for Manor Cottages at Selneston in Sussex." He assured me it would take me at least an hour and told me to be there around 10 P.M. Before I could ask for more specific directions to his house proper, Alex had hung up. I called back fifteen minutes later, but he had already left. I then telephoned train information and discovered that I would have to change trains at least once and couldn't possibly get back to London the same night. Still, I thought, Walpurgis Night comes but once a year, so I decided to splurge: I called a taxi company and ordered a cab to pick me up at eight o'clock. I figured that would give me plenty of time to sit around and gossip with Alex and Maxine before we went into the business of the ritual.

Promptly at eight a young cab driver called for me, and we were on our way. As we passed the outskirts of London, the light drizzle which had been with us all afternoon turned into a heavy rain, accompanied by fog. For April, that wasn't unusual weather, and in a way it underlined the mood of the night's adventure. But it made driving a little more difficult, and after a while the cab driver inquired whether I knew how to get to the place I was going. I informed him that I had no idea, so he proceeded to pull the car over to the curb and study his map. After about fifteen minutes, we were again on our way. Gradually the countryside was upon us, and town after town whizzed by. Yet after an hour and a half of steady driving we were nowhere near the town of Berwick, where I had intended to ask further directions from the locals. By the time we rolled into the sleepy town, it was already quarter to ten, and I began to worry lest the ritual start without me. Fortunately, I managed to get additional information at the railroad station, and we were on our way again. I recalled the telephone exchange given to me by Alex, and suddenly a road sign flashed by me with the name of that exchange on it. So I knew we could not be too far away. How close, however, I had no idea, and since British rural telephone exchanges encompass wide areas at times, we might be as little as five minutes away, or as much as an hour. By now the driver and I had one thing in common: neither of us knew exactly where we were, nor where Alex's house was located. I cautioned the driver to go a little slower, so that we might look for some road signs indicating Selneston, the village nearest Alex's house. It was quite dark by now, and I began to wonder whether I would ever get to Alex in time for the ritual, or, for that matter, at all.

The weather wasn't helping any, and by this time nothing was visible except the lights of a few houses and some wind-blown trees. I felt as if fate had decided that I should not meet Alex for the ritual after all, and for some reason fate had also decided to take me on a wild ghost chase through southern England, possibly to make me appreciate the comforts of London taxicabs. As I was beginning to feel sorry for myself I suddenly felt an electric flash go through me. Before I could think it out, I said to the driver, "Quickly, pull up at that inn over there!" I looked out of the window, and sure enough there was an inn on the right side of the road. He brought the car to a screeching halt and I jumped out. "I'm going to make inquiries inside," I said to the driver, trying to explain my strange behavior.

I shook the rain off my coat and went directly to the bar, which occupied the center portion of the pub. I had to wait on line, since several patrons wanted to be served. When the barmaid finally waited on me, I said, "I'm looking for Manor Cottages, Selneston," expecting her to say, "Oh, my, you've come the wrong way," or, "I haven't the faintest," but to my surprise she smiled and said, "You wouldn't be looking for Mr. Alex Sanders, by any chance?"

To say that I was dumbfounded is an understatement. How would she know whom I was looking for in the first place, and how would I know to stop at this unknown country pub to ask directions of someone who wasn't in a position to give them to me? Before I could say anything, she motioned me to follow her, for she had evidently guessed that her assumption had been correct. I followed her to the rear of the pub. There, comfortably ensconced in a chair behind the table and surrounded by several members of his coven, was Alexander Sanders, High Priest and "King" of the witches.

A tall glass of wine in front of him, he sat there in splendor, wearing the most bizarre dress I'd ever seen him in, with all sorts of necklaces around his neck. To his right sat Maxine, pretty as ever, and to his left three or four young people, more modestly dressed, who had apparently come along to take part in the ritual. Alex rose and greeted me. I asked him how it was that he was in this pub at this time, when we had agreed that I should go to his house directly. Alex shrugged. "I knew you were coming this way, and I decided to meet you." But I knew very well that it was his psychic will that had penetrated my mind at the critical moment and that it was he who had made me order the cab to stop in front of the pub and go inside to inquire. I accepted this without the slightest misgiving or even surprise, for I knew very well how powerful Alex can be.

We went outside, into my taxi and a private car, and drove on to Alex and Maxine's country home. There we retired to the large living room of the house and seated ourselves around the fireplace. I waited patiently for the ritual to begin, but all I got was conversation. By now it was eleven o'clock and I was wondering what Alex had in mind. Of course, I had to tell the driver that we would be back in London a little later than originally planned. By now he was beginning to get the drift of what I was up to and became interested himself.

I learned that Alex and Maxine had already performed the ordinary ritual prior to my arrival and had something very special in mind for later. I'd seen the regular ritual many times and didn't mind missing it, but when Alex told me they were going to go out into the country to do an outdoor ritual, I became somewhat worried. It was still raining and quite cold. But that didn't seem to bother Alex. Around midnight we piled into the cars again and drove to the foot of a steep mountain. Dimly visible in the distance was the white outline of the famous "Long Man of Wilmington," a prehistoric rock engraving put there by who knows what people, so large that it could be properly viewed only from the air!

We left the highway at this point and started to trudge up a narrow and very stony path, first through the fields, and then up an increasingly steep mountainside. The driver remained with his cab, but he was promised he would see the lights of the operation from where he was. There were perhaps ten or twelve of us now, mainly younger people, and Alex, wearing a black and gold robe, had gone ahead to prepare for the special fire ritual at the top of the mountain. I managed to walk up halfway, but then the darkness and the slippery path took their toll; since I have occasional bouts with vertigo, I began to feel quite uncomfortable. But the others encouraged me to go on, and when I tried to light my torch, Maxine came over and advised me to put it out again, since I could see better in the dark. She was right, and after a while I resumed my climb. Eventually I made it to the foot of the "Long Man of Wilmington." At the base, the foot was about a yard long, and one could comfortably walk up the sculpture's leg. There I halted, refusing to go any further. I had visions of rolling down the mountainside through the mud. With the encouragement of Maxine, who spoke to me through the darkness, and the excitement of what lay ahead, I managed to hold on and wait. Eventually I saw Alex appear at the top of the mountain, standing on the head of the "Long Man of Wilmington" with two lovely attendants. They were dressed in splendid long robes, and after a moment Alex began the fire ritual. It was a sort of religious dance in which the two girls helped Alex perform the ritual of the rising sun. By now it was three o'clock in the morning and the real sun would soon be up. Half an hour later, Alex and the two girls came down the mountain and joined the rest of us. He seemed elated and not at all tired. We drove back to his country house and had tea—the English answer to almost anything from tiredness to upsets. I bade the Alexander Sanderses farewell, took back to the city with me in the cab three of the young people who had come to the ritual from London, and around five o'clock checked in at the Hotel Cadogan.

I don't think the cab driver will ever forget that night; nor, for that matter, will I. But that is how it is when you go ghost-hunting or visiting witches in England. You never know how you'll spend the night.

1

GHOST-HUNTING
IN LONDON

You've got to meet Ian Adam," Elizabeth Byrd wrote the minute she heard of my intention to visit London again in pursuit of ghosts and psychic phenomena. Elizabeth is the author of many historical novels and *A Strange and Seeing Time,* in which she recounts some of her own psychic adventures. She is an expatriate American who has become something of an authority on Scotland, perhaps because of her novel, *Immortal Queen,* the story of Mary Queen of Scots. Elizabeth and I first met because of the Jumel Mansion in New York City. She was doing an article about the ghosts at Jumel and had come across my account of the colonial mansion in Washington Heights and wondered whether I would join her in investigating it further. From that sprang a long and deep friendship, and when Elizabeth moved to Scotland for good—or should I say, for better—we visited with each other every time I was overseas.

I had explained to Elizabeth that I needed someone to help me get around London, and I would be grateful for any suggestions, as well as the names of any exciting new mediums or psychic individuals I hadn't yet met. Even though I have kept in constant contact with the leading British psychics, I am forever on the lookout for potential new talent. To my surprise and pleasure, Elizabeth informed me that she had just the person for me, a gentleman friend who might help me get around London and who happened to be very psychic—Ian Adam. Elizabeth wrote me: "On Sunday night, September 17, 1972, Alanna Knight took me to visit Ian Adam, whom I had never met. After dinner he told me that he had seen two people with me at the table in the kitchen, in a haze. But when the haze lifted gradually, he minutely described one of them as my mother, even to the bright blue dress she wore and a rhinestone belt. It so happened she had bought that dress and belt and the latter was stolen at the nursing home where she died. The next night, we went out to dinner, and as we walked to the restaurant, Ian said, 'The same lady is with us, walking with a cane, wearing a bright blue coat.' My mother had to use a cane for the last five years, and the coat matched the dress. Then, two days later, as I said good-bye to him in his hall, he said suddenly, 'Don't worry about your mother; she is very happy across there, working with children; very very busy helping them to adjust.'

"Lest anyone accuse Ian of having read my mind, may I say that my mother is rarely on my mind, because her last years were too sad. However, after an accident in 1960, she complained of loneliness in her large apartment. Knowing her love of children I suggested that as she had once worked at the Medical Center, just four blocks away, she might arrange to volunteer a few afternoons a week for ambulatory young patients to come to her for cookies, milk and stories. However, she turned the suggestion down, feeling that it might complicate her life. Perhaps she is trying to make up in the world across for what she failed to do here. Ian, of course, knew nothing about my mother."

Evidently Ian Adam was a man of considerable psychic talent, although strictly on a personal and non-professional basis. "He is not a trance medium, though he often forgets what he has stated during his 'impressions,' " Elizabeth explained. "He seems wide awake as he speaks. One night I brought a stranger who had just been introduced to me by a friend to Ian's home. Ian was exhausted and said, 'I'll just have a cigarette with you and go up to sleep. Stay on and have a drink.' But Ian stayed with us two and a half hours. The incredibility is that he saw a blue haze around Allan, and asked, 'Why do you go into the desert alone, without water or petrol?' To my surprise, Allan admitted to suicidal impulses in the Sahara."

As soon as I had settled into my suite at the Hotel Cadogan, I rang Ian Adam. He promised to come over just as soon as he could disengage himself from a music lesson he was giving at the time. In addition to teaching singing, Ian operates a successful restaurant, which leaves him a good deal of time to pursue other interests, including ghost-hunting.

He turned out to be a slightly built young man who looked about thirty, with vivid eyes and a precise, responsible manner.

"You know of course about Oscar Wilde, don't you?" he said, the minute he arrived at my hotel. I assured him that I knew very well that I was staying at the same hotel where Oscar Wilde had been arrested on charges of homosexuality. In fact, I had unsuccessfully tried to get the same room Wilde had been in at the time. However, the hotel had not been altered a great deal since the nineteenth century, and thus the atmosphere was pretty much the same as it had been then. Of course, multiple layers of new impressions might have obscured the original imprint of tragedy, but apparently there was enough left in the present-day atmosphere to touch the sensitivity of Ian Adam.

Ian sat down with me in the comfortable sitting room and we ordered tea. The older part of the hotel had originally been Lord Cadogan's town house, to which a second private dwelling had been added some years later, making it into the present hotel. The bar downstairs was named the Lily Langtry. I found this more than significant, since the ghost of the famous singer, who had been a close friend of Lord Cadogan, was the first investigation on my list.

"Do you always get impressions of a psychic nature when you walk into a house?" I began the conversation.

"Not always. I think one has to be in a state of mind to receive, and often I am in that state. I may be very tired and still get the most marvelous impressions, or I can be in the wrong state of mind and get nothing. I always had this ability, even as a child, but I've had more of it during the last few years. Maybe it is because I am more willing now to listen to it."

At an early age Ian took an interest in music. His mother sang and his father played the violin and collected phonograph records of the great singers: Melchior, Tetrazzini, Caruso.

"I became a singer and sang on television and with the Scottish Opera. I've also done many recordings with the Ambrosian Singers. At present I am concentrating on doing concert work and hope eventually to get back to opera. I am being led into the musical field in a sort of inspirational way, but somehow I am always blocked at the last minute."

Since he lived but a few blocks away, Ian asked me to come over and have a look at his house. It turned out to be a lovely small house with a romantic garden in the back, almost like an opera set, filled with books, manuscripts, and knickknacks. I was particularly impressed with the well-preserved staircase leading from the ground floor to the main floor above. "I've seen the great Irish singer John McCormack on these stairs, dressed up to go to a performance," Ian explained. "It happened not long after we moved to the house. My father and mother came to live in London, and my first impression was that I met someone on the stairs, and I didn't know who it was, but I just couldn't walk past it. I couldn't see it, but I couldn't walk past it. Then I stood aside and the impression went away. But a short time later my mother said, 'You know, there is someone definitely in this house; I can feel him very often, as though he is looking down the stairs.' I tried my best to talk her out of it, so that she wouldn't feel frightened."

"What about the ghost of John McCormack?"

"Oh, it developed until he became quite clear. At the time I was studying for a song recital at Leighton House, and it was my first London recital, so it was very important to me. During the experience, my mother passed away. I found it very difficult to cope with my life at the time, but I had tremendous help from some unseen force. It may well have been him. I felt his presence more and more. One day I was working with a friend in the opera company, and afterwards she turned to me and said, 'You know, I've never heard you sing so beautifully. It wasn't your voice tonight at all.' She wasn't being disparaging in any way, but had simply noticed the difference in my voice. 'You know, you almost became a singer I had heard before, and you kept lapsing into an Irish accent.'"

The following afternoon, Ian was ready to accompany me to any of the potential hauntings I had chosen. Our first target was 103 Alexandra Road, Northwest. This was the address of what had been Lily Langtry's last home. I had learned of the location through an article in the London *Evening Standard*, dated April 2, 1965. According to this article, tables were banging in the night and voices heard whispering in a house in Alexandra Road, St. John's Wood. People in the house and the neighborhood were convinced that this was due to the ghost of Lily Langtry, the celebrated actress and beauty of the Edwardian era.

According to the *Standard*, "She lived at Leighton House as it was called for a number of years. It is said she built a glass corridor connecting the front door and the roadway so that King Edward VII could visit her in privacy. Now Leighton House, with its stained-glass windows and marble floors, has been earmarked for demolition to make way for a housing scheme. Mrs. Electra Yaras, a dark-haired Athenian who bought that lease of the haunted house eighteen years ago, said today, 'I am all in favor of progress, but it would be terrible if they pulled down this historic building. It has so many memories. Lily Langtry's ghost appeared one day at my bedroom door and asked if I would like to have a baby boy. Some time later my son was born in that very room, her old boudoir.' "

According to the *Evening Standard* reporter, Mrs. Yaras, then thirty-nine years old, was the stepdaughter of Greek General Pangalos and had several encounters with the ghostly actress.

"I woke to see a book I was reading banging up and down on the bedside table," she is quoted as saying. Her husband awoke too. "Both of us were powerless to move. But I had become used to her visits now. It was with her approval that I converted the stables of Leighton House into a studio. I've seen her vanish over the garden rockery into a misty cloud."

For three years I had tried in vain to reach Mrs. Yaras, in order to learn firsthand what her experiences had been. Her telephone had been disconnected and no forwarding address had been left. Under the circumstances I decided to go to the house with Ian to see whether it had, in fact, been demolished. When we finally located it, we found a gaping hole between two thoroughfares, the site of a future housing development. Evidently the wreckers had already done their worst, with the builders yet to come. The great Lily

Langtry had finally been dispossessed of her home, and as to her present whereabouts, one can only guess.

Tucked away in a quiet mews just this side of Hyde Park, stands an old inn called The Grenadier. The Grenadier contains the original pewter bar and is said to be the oldest inn of its kind in London. Originally, it was the officers' mess of the Duke of Wellington and was located directly outside the barracks. During the time of King George IV, the inn was known as The Guardsman, and it was already famed for its good food and drink. According to *The Old Inns of England,* "The pub is haunted during September by the ghost of an officer who died due to flogging after being caught cheating at cards."

Since cars are not permitted in the mews, we parked several blocks away and approached the inn on foot. The place had been brought to my attention originally by Bob and Dotty Cowan, who had discovered it on one of their English journeys. Mr. Cowan is an art director for a leading advertising agency, former owner of a very haunted house near Stamford, Connecticut, and both he and his wife are experienced ghost scouts. They assured me that the pub was haunted, that they had felt a "presence," and that I should look into it if I had the opportunity. At the time of my first visit, I had the strange feeling that someone was looking over my shoulder when I was reading the menu. I put that down to the fact that the inn was very crowded at the time and that people were continually walking back and forth between the bar and the dining room to the rear. But on at least one occasion, when I turned around to the waiter, I discovered that there was no waiter there. A little later that evening, when I emerged from the washroom, I had the distinct impression that there was someone waiting there to use it after me. Again, I put this down to my natural expectancy of things ghostly, and let it pass.

Now, several years later, I was back again, this time in the company of a highly psychic individual. As we opened the door to the inn, we realized that The Grenadier was about to close. Nevertheless, I approached the bar and asked whether my friend and I could visit for about ten or fifteen minutes. People were being served their last drinks for the evening as we sat in the back room to take in whatever atmosphere we could. Ian took a chair near the fireplace and closed his eyes. "I feel there was a balcony or an alcove here at one time," he began. The clock over the bar struck eleven—closing time. "Do you feel any presences here?" I asked. Ian nodded emphatically. "There are a lot of presences here. In particular, I sense a young girl and a man, a soldier." At this point, the bartender motioned to us that time was up, so we left and stood outside the inn, waiting for the crowd to disperse. A few minutes later, both inn and mews were totally deserted, except for us. As the atmosphere cleared, Ian regained his psychic perception. I asked him what he felt about the place, and the area surrounding it.

"There was a lot of activity here that wasn't right; I mean, somebody planned a murder here and it was carried out. I am sure those who planned it were hiding around here." I pointed toward the back of a church which stood adjacent to the pub. "Yes," Ian continued,

"I can see an entirely different setting here as well, without any house. The street was much narrower. I see the area not as neat as it is now and sort of neglected. This building was connected with the church, and poor people came here. I am speaking of the late eighteenth century. I have the feeling that this was a crossover point and had something to do with soldiers and a barracks. I think they came this way on their horses and crossed down here where you're standing, and I feel a lot of traffic in this funny little road—people selling things, vendors, going right back into the seventeenth century. I have a feeling that this was known as a nasty area."

We walked a few steps and looked at the old buildings. A sign read, Old Barrack Yard. "This is it," Ian exclaimed. "Here were the barracks. I have a tremendous sense that someone was very viciously murdered here and that it had been planned."

"Are you referring to the girl or the man?" I asked, remembering what he had said inside the pub.

"I think there were three of them involved in it. I think the girl is connected with it too. But somehow I have a feeling that *I have been here before in another life.*"

"Has this ever happened to you before? I mean, somewhere else?" I asked.

"Yes," Ian nodded. "Several years ago, I was walking around Venice and I felt I knew every place, every street, every back alley. I was walking over the oldest part of the city, not a very good part, where tourists seldom go. Italians don't go there because it is the section where bodies are taken when someone dies. I was walking there, and all of a sudden I knew the place very well. I stopped in front of a little shop and went inside and asked for a lantern, a lamp for my home. The lady in the shop said, 'It is very strange that you should ask for a lamp, for we don't sell lamps. Still, I have kept two lamps here for almost forty years, and you can have them.' She explained to me that when they had taken over the shop fifty years before, the shop had indeed been selling lamps, but not since. These two lanterns were all that was left from the previous owner, and so she sold them to me. How could I have known that? Unless, of course, I had been to the shop before."

Margery Lawrence is a novelist and writer of short stories. Her most successful novel was *The Madonna of Seven Moons,* which was also made into a motion picture. Mrs. Lawrence has always maintained an interest in the psychic, and some of her fiction is based on real experiences. Married twice, she was a widow when she first contacted me in 1967. "Since my husband's death," she explained, "I've continued to maintain an interest in psychic phenomena, which is, to my mind, the most important science in the world, and the only thing that can restore mankind to sanity—if it will let it!"

Living in Inverness Terrace, Bayswater, Mrs. Lawrence offered to relate an encounter with a ghost which went back to the time when she was a teen-ager. The area where it all happened was smashed to pieces during the Blitz, but the experience was as fresh in her mind as if it had happened yesterday.

"I was studying art at the time along with others in a large studio in Chelsea. One particular night, I was planning to have supper at the flat of two friends, a young journalist and his wife. They had just rented it, and it was located in the Lambeth area, a quarter of London which was once very fashionable but which is now definitely in the slum category. Many of the fine old Victorian houses have now become boarding houses or are being split up into cheap flats, but they are still standing despite the bombing in the last war.

"After my class was over, I went off to Lambeth and found myself facing a fine old house. The door was opened to me by a rather frowsy old charwoman who was cleaning the hall. She told me my friends had gone out to buy things for supper, but they had left word for me to make myself at home in their new flat, which opened off the hall on the ground floor. I found that the flat was actually one large room split into two by sliding doors that now stood apart about one foot. The front half was used as a sitting room; the table was laid for supper, and there was a bright fire in the fireplace. I dropped my outdoor things on a chair and sat down to warm my hands at the fire, which was a large one and bright enough to light the entire room. I hadn't been sitting there more than a minute when I realized that I was not alone. I looked up and saw a stoutish middle-aged man standing on the side of the marble mantelpiece, resting one elbow on it and looking down at me with an air of mild interest. He was dressed in Dickensian sort of clothes—tight, dark-colored trousers, a red waistcoat, high black stock, and collar points rising to his cheeks, where they met thick black whiskers. He was bald on top, though I could see black hair behind his ears. I was astonished, but concluded that my friends had invited somebody to supper to meet me and vaguely concluded that he was either going on to a fancy dress party, or else was one of those eccentrics who chose to copy the dress of his forefathers. I thought he must have been in the other room, and I said something vague about being sorry that I hadn't seen him; and then, looking past him to the sliding doors, still standing far too close to each other for any normal person to come through, suddenly I knew that I was frightened! I sprang to my feet, and as I did so, the man smiled kindly at me, raised one hand in a reassuring gesture as though to say, 'It's all right; don't be scared of me,' and withdrew backwards towards the narrow gap between the sliding doors—and vanished through them!

"I rushed out into the hall and into the arms of my returning friends, to whom over supper I related my amazing experience and begged them to try and find out what story lay behind the haunting. They had only just moved in and had had no such experience themselves; but they were most interested and promised to find out what they could, and after a while, thanks to cautious questioning of the charwoman and other tenants, they found out what had happened.

"Apparently, the haunting was well known, though naturally the agent who had the job of renting the flats had said nothing about it to my friends. But the haunting only occurred on the ground floor and, as a rule, in the front room where I had been sitting. It seems that in Victorian days the house had been owned by a wealthy bookie who had a wife he adored, a pretty woman much younger than he was, but alas, one day an evil fate overtook him. Not only did he lose so much money one season over racing that he neared bankruptcy, but his wife ran off with a younger man—and as they had never had any children, he felt he had nothing left to live for and hanged himself from the giant hook in the center of the ceiling of the front room. It was the same hook from which had once hung the handsome crystal chandelier that had lighted many fine parties in his better days.

"Until then, I had thought that ghosts were wispy, transparent shapes, but this man was as solid as a real man."

The first time I met Evelyn Haley, of New York City, was when she signed up for a haunted castle tour I was organizing in conjunction with Vision Travel several years ago. There were about fifteen people in this group, chiefly women, some of whom had had psychic experiences before. Others came along out of curiosity, in the hope of experiencing something out of the ordinary. By the end of the trip, almost everybody had had some sort of psychic experience in one of the many places we were visiting. Mrs. Haley, along with several others, was assigned to the Hotel Piccadilly in London, one of the older and busier hotels in central London. The building itself showed its age, and very little had been done to it in a structural way since it was first erected. Mrs. Haley was given Room 537.

"I've been traveling to all parts of the world for many years," Mrs. Haley explained to me, "and I have occupied rooms in many hotels, but never have I experienced the sensation I had when I entered this very attractive and nicely furnished room in the Hotel Piccadilly. Immediately, I felt icy cold, and I had the impression that I could never sleep in that room. I went into the spacious and well-appointed bathroom to wash my hands. As I stood there, I had the feeling that I wasn't alone. I turned and saw the bathroom door closing slowly all by itself. Just at that moment, the bellboy brought my luggage and I dashed downstairs to join the rest of the group for dinner.

"I explained to Andre Michalski of the travel agency that I couldn't possibly stay in that room. Very graciously he said that he would have my room changed. A gentleman from San Francisco, who said that he was a sensitive, offered to go into the room with me after dinner to see what impressions he might receive. The rest of the group waited out in the hall until he came out of the room. He explained that he felt very distinctly that a person had died in the bathtub as a result of cutting her wrists. The hotel moved me to a dismal inside room across the hall. It was poorly furnished and, I also felt, too near the original room, but I was too embarrassed to ask for yet another change.

"Later on that night, when I returned to the hotel, I had a feeling that something was waiting for me in the hall. I went into my dreary room, locked and bolted the hall door and climbed into bed to read. Opposite my bed there was a wardrobe. Suddenly the closed door of the wardrobe opened all by itself. I got up and closed it, but in a few minutes the same thing happened again. After getting up several times to close the door, I became annoyed and shouted, 'Stop that!' Immediately the door stopped half open. When I closed it again, it remained closed.

"After I had just dropped off to sleep, I was awakened by the very loud sound of water gushing full force out of the taps in the bathroom, which was only about five feet to the right of my bed. I had left the door ajar. Sleepily, I climbed out of bed and started toward the bathroom, when the noise stopped, so I fell back into bed and continued sleeping. In the morning when I picked up my watch and prepared to wind it, as was my custom, something told me that it had been wound already, and sure enough I found it to be fully wound. Then, much to my surprise, upon leaving the room I found that the door had been unlocked from the inside, both by key and bolt. After that I could feel something touching me very gently, but I had no other remarkable manifestations. I had asked her to behave herself, and apparently she was obedient."

Ghosts are taken quite seriously in England. A woman and her two children had to move out of an eighty-year-old home because it was built over a three-hundred-year-old burial ground for plague victims, in Croydon, near London. According to newspaper reports, Mrs. Mary Wild had been thrilled to move into the house with her daughter Janet, then ten, and son Charles, two, but their lives soon turned into nightmares. "During our first night there, Janet heard footsteps and came into bed with me," she is quoted as complaining. "Then something pulled the sheets off us and Janet was thrown out of bed. We pushed a heavy chest of drawers in front of the door, but it was moved aside." It was then that Mrs. Wild learned that several previous tenants had left the house after staying only a few weeks. During the one-month period she managed to stay at the house, she heard all sorts of noises, footsteps, and sounds of something dragging a sack along the floor. She has also heard a clock tick, even though there isn't a clock in the flat and a dog barking when there is no dog. Vases turned upside down and screams added to the terror of the haunting. Finally, the deputy housing manager, one Stanley Stratton, referred the matter to the local medical officer. It was then discovered that the house had been built over the Waddon Marshes, an unofficial burial ground where plague victims had been buried in the past.

Mrs. Kathleen Reeves, a divorcee, travels a good deal, even to Pennsylvania, trying to discover what life is all about. Her ex-husband works for a local newspaper and she makes her home in and around Wanstead, which is just outside London proper. Ever since she heard me on the BBC, she has been writing to me about this and that psychic experience, hoping to meet me sometime to tell me more about them. Twice she missed me while passing through New York City on her way to her Pennsylvania friends. But in April, 1973, we finally caught up with each other in London at the Hotel Cadogan. Over high tea, she tried to sort it all out. Unfortunately, many of her experiences were of a very slight nature, but there were some chilling incidents I'd like to share with my readers.

When she was still living at home with her parents, at Bartlow near Cambridge, Mrs. Reeves had an eerie experience. It happened about half-past twelve, near an old railroad line. She and her mother saw an aged railroad guard they both knew well walk across the rails

as if going to his train. When they got home, Mrs.
Reeves remarked to her father that they had seen that
certain railroad man, but her father immediately replied that they couldn't have, because that particular
man wasn't on duty that day. Kathleen insisted, however, and her mother backed her up. Two days later
they found out that the man had been dying at his own
home at the moment they had both seen him go to his
job.

Then there was the lodger who fell in love with her
when she was living in an old house in Sudbury. Although the man was very much in love with Kathleen,
she could not return his feelings. She left Sudbury a
year later, not caring how Mr. Nicholson, the lodger,
would take it. Some years after that, she found herself
on a bus to Blackheath and was preparing to get off at
a certain stop. As she looked out of the window, to her
amazement she saw Mr. Nicholson standing in the
street, looking at her. She was so surprised she forgot to
get off, and the bus went on. Not much later she happened to be back in Sudbury, and on a hunch she went
to the local pharmacy, where Mr. Nicholson used to
work, and inquired after him. It seems he had died the
very day she had seen him standing at the bus stop!

Joan Randall is a writer of romantic fiction and
occasional articles in such magazines as *Prediction.* Her
psychic experiences go back a long way, and one particular incident stands out in her memory. This was during World War II, when she was a child. Her mother
had admonished the children that if the sirens started,
they should go next door into the neighbor's basement.

One afternoon her mother went into town to do some shopping. Sure enough, the sirens went off, and, as her mother hadn't returned, Joan went to the house to get books and comics, as kids do. As she did so, she saw her mother standing in front of the house.

"What in the world are you doing?" Joan said to her mother. "Come on, the siren is going, mother! Hurry up!"

"But my mother walked into the house and then disappeared completely. Later, when my mother returned from shopping, I discussed it with her. It appears that she had tried to get into a shelter in town, but the warden had come up and said, 'I'm sorry, we're all full in here; you have to go to the one down the road,' so mother ran off, with shrapnel falling everywhere. The next thing she heard was a loud explosion, and everybody in the shelter she hadn't gotten into was killed outright. It was at that exact moment she heard my voice, calling out to her."

Not long ago Miss Randall had a strange dream, if that is what it was. She saw herself in a very old house looking at a picture of a man she thought she ought to know, and then she heard someone say, "This is Sir Arthur Conan Doyle," and she heard herself reply, "Oh, really? I've never met him at all," and at that moment he stepped from his picture. He said to her, "Whatever you do, don't try to get to me, and don't meddle too deeply in the occult, unless you are sure of what you are doing, because you might get possessed."

"I woke up at this point," Miss Randall explained, "and I saw him standing by the bed. Then he disappeared. The following day I got a book out of the library, and there was the exact picture of the man I had seen. Until that moment I had no idea he was involved in spiritualism or the occult."

By a strange set of circumstances I got to know Dave Clark, the famous pop singer whose Dave Clark Five group is well known in the music world. A friend in Pittsburgh had had recurrent dreams in which she saw herself looking for Dave Clark, because she and he were somehow linked in a previous life. She wasn't sure in what capacity they had known each other, but she had a compulsion to find out for herself, and she kept asking me to make contact with Dave Clark for her, since it was more likely I would be able to get through to the famous singer. Eventually I went to London, and having written ahead to Dave Clark, I hoped he would respond. When I did not receive any call from him or his manager, I telephoned the manager myself and asked that Mr. Clark call me back as soon as he could. I had almost given up hope that Clark would call me, feeling that he probably considered me simply a fan, when he rang me back.

Clark turned out to be a soft-spoken, kindly man quite interested in psychic matters. I explained briefly why I wanted to see him, but he had just been in a recording session and was quite tired. But he called me the following day and invited me to his apartment to discuss the matter further.

When I arrived at his penthouse on Curzon Street, I was received by Clark and a friend, a young singer from Australia named Johnny. Unfortunately, Dave Clark did not recall any recurrent dreams of the kind my Pittsburgh friend had reported to me: try as he would he could not picture himself knowing her in a previous life. But the occult was by no means a strange subject to Dave Clark. Some years earlier he had found himself in a motion picture theater with some friends. Suddenly, he was gripped by unreasonable fear and wanted to leave the theater immediately. For several minutes he was almost unable to control his panic, having a strong desire to leave the group and run outside, but he realized that such strange behavior might upset his friends, so he stayed on. After a few minutes, the feeling passed as abruptly as it had come. As soon as he got home, however, he received a telephone call from his parents. "You almost lost us tonight," his mother said, and went on to explain that she and Dave's father had very nearly been swept out to sea by a huge wave. When Clark asked the time when this had occurred, he discovered that it was at the exact moment when the stark fear had overcome him in the movie theater.

When he needed help concerning a growth, he went to see the spiritual healer, Ted Fricker. At that time Clark was an unknown, trying to break into show business. Fricker put his hands on Clark's jaw and promised that the growth would disappear. He also inquired after the young singer's interests, and when he heard that Clark was trying to break into the big time as a popular singer, he offered to introduce him to another patient of his, a man whom he had recently cured of blindness. The following day the growth had entirely disappeared.

Not much later, Clark became a big name in show business. Later he met the formerly blind producer of whom Fricker had spoken. The producer admitted, sheepishly, that he had been approached by Fricker about Clark, but had dismissed the matter as just another attempt by someone to help a friend. In retrospect the producer realized that he could have headlined Clark a lot sooner had he followed the healer's advice.

2
GREAT BRITISH MEDIUMS

If England is the ancestral home of all ghosts, as popular belief would have it, then it would seem that she is also home to the best mediums in the world. This is partially true, in that the *standards* of mediumship are more carefully observed in England than they are in the United States. Of course, there are fraudulent mediums in England, and there are honest and reputable mediums in every other country in the world. But, by and large, what is considered professional ethics differs greatly between England and the United States. For one thing, English and Scottish mediums do not require approval from government authorities, as they do in the United States, where many states demand that a psychic individual who wishes to pursue a career as a professional medium become a religious minister. As a result, we have a number of reverends in the United

States who can barely write and read and whose religious attitudes do not conform to even the lowest denominational standards. We have self-appointed bishops with congregations of one who advertise in various newspapers and magazines, and churches consisting only of storefronts; we have cults that worship the devil but which, nevertheless, come under the legal designation of church, and their leaders are considered ministers with the title of reverend. None of this foolishness exists in the United Kingdom. To begin with, mediums are not interfered with in their work unless they are patently fraudulent and someone complains. Even then, proof must be given that money has changed hands and that a tangible fraud has in fact been perpetrated. Accusation alone is no longer sufficient, as it was in the Middle Ages, to convict a person possessed of so-called supernatural powers.

The majority of tested, respectable professional mediums give private sittings at the headquarters of the Spiritualist Association of Great Britain, 33 Belgrave Square, or at the College of Psychic Studies, 16 Queensbury Place, South West. There is, of course, a large number of independent mediums throughout the United Kingdom who are reached directly and individually, some with Spiritualist leanings and others without. There is an entire spectrum of psychic professionals ranging all the way from trance mediums to simple clairvoyants. Some individuals combine psychic gifts with astrology; others, with the more intuitive processes of psychic insight, read tarot cards or crystal balls. To the best of my knowledge, none of these responsible individuals have ever charged exorbitant fees. There are a few so-called Gypsy tea-leaf-readers in England, though not nearly so many as in the United States. A Gypsy tea-leaf-reader is not necessarily either a Gypsy or a tea-leaf-reader, though some of them are, and some are even quite talented in terms of psychic ability. But the majority of these individuals, whether working in organized chains of tea rooms or as individuals out of their own homes, are not really possessed of any special gift except the ability to make money from unsuspecting, naïve individuals in need of advice.

The truly great mediums in England are always in demand, and sittings with them must be booked well in advance. Those who have been publicized in the press or through books, such as Ena Twigg, are almost unapproachable. I recall the difficulty I had seeing Ena the last time I was in London, not because she was unwilling to sit with me, but because she had apportioned her time so far in advance she couldn't fit me in. There is always, of course, the danger that too much publicity gives a medium a big head and fills her with the illusion that she is no longer simply a channel of communication but some sort of prophetic authority. When this happens, the usefulness of the medium suffers inevitably, even though her fame may rise to unprecedented heights. As I see it, the best mediums are those who do not change over the years, who do not go out of their way to explain themselves to anyone, who do not seek the glaring publicity of television or newspaper interviews, but continue to do that for which they are best suited—namely, individual sittings with responsible individuals, occasional public sittings, and work with researchers, if they are qualified and they are requested to do so. To do otherwise might put a premium on successful discharge of psychic duties: evidential mediumship should be not the exception but the norm. Substandard performance is unacceptable; psychic individuals who render services at this level would be better off in other professions.

My way of testing the efficiency of mediums is simple. I book myself with the medium I want to test, sometimes giving only initials or another name, and I do not divulge anything about myself. The medium with whom I sit has no way of knowing who I am, except perhaps that I am an American, judging by my clothes and accent. If the results of such a sitting are satisfactory and the material of the kind that cannot be explained by foreknowledge of my circumstances by the medium, then I consider the medium an impressive one.

E. D. B. is a professional management consultant in California, well established, a self-described conservative Republican, a Rotarian, and, in his own words, not young. When he contacted me in the summer of 1971, he explained that the question of afterlife had not interested him very much, since one is dead soon enough and will find out at that time whether there is life after death. Mr. B. and his wife were waiting at the airport en route to Europe when he happened to pick up one of my books containing the names and addresses of several English mediums. Shortly after his arrival in London he decided to go to a sitting with Mrs. Betty Wakeling at the College of Psychic Studies.

The sitting proceeded well, with all sorts of bits and

pieces of an evidential nature coming through for Mr. and Mrs. B. All of a sudden the medium said, "There is a gentleman here whose last name is James. He wants to make it clear it is his surname, not his Christian name. He is very interested in you. Do you know him?"

Mr. B. immediately thought of an English business associate who had died about ten years before and whose name was D. S. James. He acknowledged this message, and the medium went on to talk about Mr. James's using a computing machine of some sort.

"This made no sense to me," Mr. B. explained to me, "because good old Jimmy James was one of the world's great salesmen, with little interest in desk work or mathematical analysis. We sparred around with this for a while, when Mrs. B. whispered to me, 'You knew *two* Jameses.' Of course I did. A. S. James died four and a half years ago. He was a certified public accountant who handled that phase of the work for the company I ran until 1963 and with whom I had other business. I had completely forgotten the American James, perhaps because we were in England. After the identity crisis had passed, we had an interesting and humorous conversation with my old accountant, who, according to the sensitive, is still doing something like this for me."

There are about half a dozen mediums regularly in attendance at the Spiritualist Association of Great Britain and at the College of Psychic Studies. At the Spiritualist headquarters, the most outstanding mediums in terms of evidence are Ivy Jaggers, of whom I have written elsewhere, and a Welshman named Roy Morgan, who never ceases to amaze me with the accuracy of his psychic readings, with the number of names and amount of data he is able to produce. No vagueness or pastoral consolation from him, but precise data, much of it pertaining to the future, some of it to the past.

I last sat with him on April 30, 1973; by then he knew who I was, although we do not keep in touch with each other, and he hasn't read any of my books. He simply remembered my face and my name. Nevertheless, anything he might "get from me" that was also found in my published books would have to be discounted. Any other details, especially private matters, would have to be judged purely on merit. For instance, he described where I lived in New York, that it was near water, that I lived on a high floor and had a lovely view of the river, that I was married to a Countess, and that one of my two children would be very good at ballet—all of it correct. Morgan also saw me doing a radio show, something which only came true in January of the following year. He also spoke of some relatives of mine he felt present and mentioned their names: Oscar, Otto, and Henry. It so happens that Oscar was a cousin, while Otto and Henry were, respectively, a brother and an uncle of mine. He mentioned the name Franz and immediately connected it with the name Herman. A beloved teacher of mine who had passed away some years before was named Franz, and one of his sons is called Herman. He talked about a family house in a place called Brno in which the three relatives he had named were living at one time. He described the house and the grounds and added two more names, Lydia and Rudi. In the first place, a Welshman is not likely to know of the city of Brno in Czechoslovakia, and in any case he could not easily have guessed my connection with it. The two additional names also fit, being related both to each other and to me. According to Mr. Morgan, all these dead relatives were standing around us when he was speaking of them.

Richard Gardner is an independent medium who gives private sittings by arrangement and whose methods of divination are unique in the sense that he has created techniques not quite like anyone else's.

"I am very much interested in raising what is subconscious onto the level of consciousness," he explained, "and integrating it with the more familiar conscious mind. As we evolve further, the whole molecular structure of the cells changes, giving us a body no longer subject to death or decay." Mr. Gardner was implying that we could actually conquer death. "I think we die now because we don't know what we are doing. We are frequently going against the cosmic flow and suffer as a result. I think this is the meaning of the phrase, 'The wages of sin is death.'"

Mr. Gardner uses a special deck of twelve cards designed for him by Tammo de Jongh. He does readings by inviting a subject to select three or four of the cards, and from these selections he judges a great deal about the person's true self. In a book entitled *The Purpose of Life*, Richard Gardner has set down the twelve functions or consciousnesses which these cards represent. "The tarot cards represent composite entities, while my cards represent only a function, not a person," he explained.

"Do you foretell the future from these cards?" I asked.

Mr. Gardner smiled an enigmatic Irish smile. "They say I do. But I also use the tarot to complement my readings. I can show clients which functions among the twelve are too strong in them and which they would need to contemplate. It is a sobering realization, because we are often complaining about what life is doing to us, when in fact we are playing a large part in it. When a client begins to cultivate a function he has not been using, a lot of changes occur."

"How exactly do you work with these cards?"

"I find that the subconscious responds better to symbols than to the written word, so when I am looking at these pictures in the cards, they activate my psychic aspect."

"When you see things in the cards, are those unalterable facts that will occur or trends that *might* happen?"

"They are more often trends, in the sense that we are all on some sort of road. There is always a choice if the client is equal to changing his ways."

"Are you saying that the event itself will definitely occur, but the outcome is indefinite?"

"Yes. One gets moments of choice. He can do something about his pattern."

"If you were to read a person again after a while would you see this?"

"Yes, I have seen people change."

"You have written a number of books on your method, I believe?"

"The first book was *Evolution Through the Tarot,* in which I penetrated as deeply as I could into the symbolism of the twenty-two major arcana. Then there was a demand for a fortune-telling kind of book, so I wrote another one, *The Tarot Speaks.* Finally, I got together with three other people—a mathematician, an artist, and an historian—and we worked for about eight years trying to discover the aspects of consciousness which we either use or neglect. I found this a striking breakthrough in the understanding of human behavior, so I wrote a book which is called, *The Purpose of Life."*

"I recall when we first met some years ago you told me that you were originally building houses in Ireland. How did you get involved with the occult?"

"My mother discovered my special ability when I was quite small. She asked me what would hapen if she did such and such a thing, and I apparently told her accurately. By the time I reached twenty-one the gift had disappeared. But I became interested in palmistry, which I had tried since age eleven, and it seems that reading tarot cards brought out my psychic talents again. Circumstances forced me to go professional. I didn't much like staying in Ireland building houses all the time, and I didn't like the business world. I found it too harsh and unfeeling, and the rewards did nothing for the heart. I found the kind of contact that happens between people in a psychic circumstance a much more real and helpful situation, both to the recipient and to the one who is supposed to be helping him."

"Aren't you also an initiated witch?"

"Indeed, I am," Mr. Gardner replied proudly. "I was initiated into the Gardnerian form of witchcraft— no relation, by the way. To me, witchcraft means the worship of the great feminine principle in the cosmos, as opposed to the worshipping of the great masculine principle, as practiced in other religions. Once in a while I visit various witch covens and take part in the rituals."

Two years ago Richard Gardner suffered a slight heart attack and has been living in the south of England ever since. He can be reached by writing to 10 Sudeley Street, Brighton, Sussex. The special cards, with explanatory notes on how to use them, are also obtainable through Mr. Gardner.

Ronald Hearn has made quite a reputation for himself as a clairvoyant and trance medium of late. When I met him several years ago he had been recommended to me by the College of Psychic Studies, and since I was then investigating the haunting at the Gargoyle Club in Soho, I brought Mr. Hearn to the nightclub, without of course telling him why or even where he was going. While he was in deep trance, the disturbed spirit of Nell Gwyn communicated through him, giving rather startling evidence of her life on earth. Since that time, Ronald Hearn has apparently developed new methods for his private readings, and I questioned him about them.

"I take a letter requesting a sitting or a reading, and just from the letter I get impressions which I put on a tape recorder; then I send them the tape. Actually, I don't even touch the letter. I simply tune in to the person I am reading for and ask that the Other Side supply me with information."

"Then it is not psychometry?"* I asked.

Hearn shook his head. "No, it isn't. It is communication with the spirit world. That is why holding a letter

---

*Deriving psychic information by touching an object or person.

isn't going to make any difference as far as I'm concerned; I don't want to boost someone's uncertainties with psychological counsel. If I don't get any vibration, I can't do it. Sometimes I give the readings without having a letter. Often, I've only met them afterwards. All of these readings are by mail, and I think there must be about eighteen hundred of them to date."

Hearn claims that 95 percent of his readings by mail are accurate, and he has many clients in America as well. They have heard of him through stories in the *Psychic News*, the weekly which has headlined him several times. Hearn has been to the United States four times, lecturing on his work and giving private readings. But he hasn't done any work with haunted houses since our collaboration a few years back. Nor has the British Society for Psychical Research ever asked for his help. Mr. Hearn, a lively man in his thirties, is not exactly shy about his abilities. "I do psychometry and of course demonstrate clairvoyance during my lectures. Sometimes I do trance work; I train people; I do healings—you name it. I probably cover quite a few of the aspects."

He has a spirit guide during his trance work, but he doesn't worry about what might happen when he is, so to speak, "out."

"I have implicit trust. I believe that working with the spirit world is a question of cooperation. I make my demands of them, as I believe they make of me, and I think if we work together and respect each other, I don't see why anything should go wrong."

Mr. Hearn has been a medium for a number of years now. Originally he was an auditor for the British government, a job he described as "very uninspiring, and, though responsible, very boring." At first, when he discovered his gift, Hearn worked as a part-time medium, doing his job during the day and spending evenings and weekends as a psychic. But as word got around about his ability, the demand became so heavy he had to quit his daytime job.

"When I was twenty-five I went to a psychic reader and received a message that I was a psychic. I argued very strongly against it, because I had never had any psychic impression in my life up to then. The idea of being a psychic was quite ridiculous to me, but the little lady who gave me the reading insisted that not only was I psychic, but I would go on to become one of the best-known mediums in the world. I thought this quite hilarious, but this lady, Mrs. Blenkiron, insisted that she was right. She was working at a local Spiritualist church. I had originally gone to her because a man in the local pub where I used to meet my friends talked about her. That first time when I went to her church, I knew nothing about the work and wanted to find out more about it. Mrs. Blenkiron said to me, 'There is a man standing beside you. He is wearing a schoolmaster's cap and gown. He says his name is Harry. He is your grandfather.' Well, all my relatives had passed over before I was born. Consequently, I had not heard anything about them, except for a grandfather who had been a schoolteacher by the name of Harry. I found the medium fascinating. Then she reeled off a whole lot more information about my relatives, but I said, 'I'm sorry, I don't know any of them.' When I got home I asked my mother about them, and the medium had been dead right. I was impressed. Until that evening, I had never seen the medium before, and she had never seen me. I scarcely knew anything about the subject, so where did she get all the information? To me, that was a challenge. I went back again and again for more information, only to be told each time, 'Why, you are a psychic yourself.' One day a man in my office looked at me and asked, 'Are you a Spiritualist?' It turned out he had felt all along that I would make a fine medium. He sent me to a friend of his, a medium, who insisted I would be a professional psychic someday. By that time I began to think that they were all mad. Still, I kept going to his little Spiritualist church, and eventually I took a developing class with Nora Blackwood, sort of as a challenge. From the very first moment I sat in her class, I went into trance without realizing it, and everything started to happen. It was my first trance experience, and an entity came through me, a North American Indian called Running Water. They recorded it, because he spoke in his own language, which meant nothing to me.

"When I opened my eyes, coming out of this trance, I thought I had fallen asleep. I felt terrible. I thought, here I had come to this class, and the very first night I fall asleep! But when I opened my eyes, the room was full of people, as real as you are at this moment, and I thought, this is peculiar. But instead of being scared out of my wits, I looked at them. I began to feel well. There had been about eighteen people in the room when we started, and there were at least double that number now. I could see one or two Indians with full headdresses and a nun and a Chinese, but some very ordinary people too, and then suddenly they all seemed to melt or vanish and I realized we had gotten to the end of the class. Nora Blackwood refused to believe that I hadn't been in a circle or class before, because I had gone into deep trance the very first time. I do remember that before I went 'to sleep,' I had this strange tingling sensation in my legs, as if a charge of electricity were going through them. I suppose that was the trance coming on. After that, it took quite a while to get it organized and workable, before I could really give communications and demonstrations, but that was the beginning."

"How did the people you saw upon awakening from the trance differ from ordinary people of the flesh-and-blood variety?"

"They didn't, really. They seemed as solid and real as anyone else in the room. They were mostly standing behind other people, I mean flesh-and-blood people."

"When you looked at them, did they look back at you?"

"Oh, yes. They seemed to be quite pleasant. They were in full color."

"Do you still see people like that?"

"No, I wish I did. This worked for quite a time. I used to have the most fantastic visions for a few months, but then in time they sort of disappeared and I received more mental impressions instead, which is the way I work now. I don't see anything at all now. I receive a feeling or impression from my mind. The impressions come through me, but from a discarnate person."

"Does your own ESP ability supply you with any information at all?"

"Well, telepathy and mind reading must enter into every sort of communication to a degree; certainly in my case, because when I was in the army I was trained by British Intelligence. I can take in a person at a glance and assess the character pretty well. But this I attribute to my own ability, not to the Other Side."

Since Mr. Hearn's mother passed away, he lives by himself. He is in regular contact with her, however. Ronald Hearn, for those who might be interested, can be reached at 9 Grove Lodge, Crescent Grove, London, SW 47 AE.

3

ROYALTY AND GHOSTS

According to the German newspaper, *Neues Zeit-alter* of April 18, 1964, Queen Elizabeth II has had a number of psychic experiences. She accepts the reality of spirit survival and maintains a lively interest in the occult. In this respect she follows in the tradition of the House of Windsor, which has always been interested in psychic phenomena. King George V, for instance, took part in seances and, after his death, communicated with noted researchers through a number of mediums, including the late Geraldine Cummins. It was the same Miss Cummins, parenthetically, who brought through some extremely evidential messages from the late President Franklin D. Roosevelt. This is not surprising, since Miss Cummins was a disciplined medium, well trained to receive intricate and detailed messages.

Whenever word of Spiritualist seances at Buckingham Palace gets out, the press has a field day, especially the British press, which displays, with rare exceptions, a singularly disrespectful attitude towards the reality of psychic phenomena. Under the circumstances one cannot blame the palace for the usual blanket denial of such rumors, even if they happen to be based on fact.

But a Frenchman by the name of François Veran claimed to have had reliable information that Spiritualist seances were taking place in Buckingham Palace and that Queen Elizabeth II had confided in friends that her late father, King George VI, had appeared to her no fewer than six times after his death. There had been a particularly close relationship between father and daughter, and prior to his death King George VI had assured his daughter he would always be with her in times of need, even from the beyond. The queen's sister, Princess Margaret, is known to be interested in psychic research, and Prince Philip, the royal consort, has lent his name as patron to a research effort by the great medical pioneer Dr. Douglas Baker, a parapsychologist and member of the College of Surgeons. This cautious involvement by members of the British royal family is not a recent inclination, however, for Queen Victoria maintained a close and continuing relationship with seers of her time, notably John Brown, who served ostensibly as the queen's gilly or orderly, but whose real attraction lay in his pronounced psychic gift, which he put at the disposal of his queen.

Nearly all the royal residences of Britain are haunted. There is a corridor in the servants' quarters of Sandringham, the castle where Queen Elizabeth II was born, where servants have frequently observed the ghost of a footman of an earlier age. There is Windsor

Castle near London, where the face of George III has appeared to witnesses, and there is the Bloody Tower of London with all its grisly memories and the ghosts of at least two queens. There may be others at the Tower, for nobody has yet had a chance to go in with a competent trance medium and ferret out all the psychic remains. British authorities, despite reputations to the contrary, take a dim view of such endeavors, and I for one have found it difficult to get much cooperation from them. Cooperation or not, the ghosts are there.

Probably the most celebrated of British royal ghosts is the shade of unlucky Queen Anne Boleyn, the second wife of Henry VIII, who ended her days on the scaffold. Accused of infidelity, which was a form of treason in the sixteenth century, she had her head cut off despite protestations of her innocence. In retrospect, historians have well established that she was speaking the truth. But at the time of her trial, it was a political matter to have her removed from the scene, and even her uncle, who sat in judgment of her as the trial judge, had no inclination to save her neck.

Anne Boleyn's ghost has been reported in a number of places connected with her in her lifetime. There is, first of all, her apparition at Hampton Court, attested to by a number of witnesses over the years, and even at Windsor Castle, where she is reported to have walked along the eastern parapet. At the so-called Salt Tower within the confines of the Tower of London, a guard observed her ghost walking along headless, and he promptly fainted. The case is on record, and the man insisted over and over again that he had not been drinking.

Perhaps he would have received a good deal of

sympathy from a certain Lieutenant Glynn, a member of the Royal Guard, who has stated, also for the record, "I have seen the great Queen Elizabeth and recognized her, with her olive skin color, her fire-red hair, and her ugly dark teeth. There is no doubt about it in my mind." Although Elizabeth died a natural death at a ripe old age, it is in the nature of ghosts that both the victims and the perpetrators of crimes sometimes become restless once they have left the physical body. In the case of good Queen Bess, there was plenty to be remorseful over. Although most observers assume Queen Elizabeth "walks" because of what she did to Mary Queen of Scots, I disagree. Mary had plotted against Elizabeth, and her execution was legal in terms of the times and conditions under which the events took place. If Queen Elizabeth I has anything to keep her restless, it would have to be found among the many lesser figures who owed their demise to her anger or cold cunning, including several ex-lovers.

Exactly as described in the popular English ballad, Anne Boleyn had been observed with "her 'ead tucked under," not only at the Tower of London, but also at Hever Castle, in Kent, where she was courted by King Henry VIII. To make things even more complicated, on the anniversary of her execution she allegedly drives up to the front door of Blickling Hall, Norfolk, in a coach driven by a headless coachman and drawn by four headless horses, with herself sitting inside holding her head in her lap. That, however, I will have to see before I believe it.

A number of people have come forward to claim, at the very least, acquaintanceship with the unlucky

Anne Boleyn in a previous life, if not identity with her. Naturally, one has to be careful to differentiate between the real thing and a romantically inclined person's fantasizing herself or himself back into another age, possibly after reading some books dealing with the period or after seeing a film. The circumstances surrounding Anne are well known; her history has been published here and abroad, and unless the claimant comes up with some hitherto unknown facet of the queen's life, or at the very least some detail that is not generally known or easily accessible in the existing literature, a prima-facie case cannot really be established.

As I am firmly convinced of the reality of reincarnation and have published two books dealing with this subject, I am perhaps in a position to judge what is a real reincarnation memory and what is not. Thus, when Mrs. Charlotte Tuton of Boston contacted me in early 1972 with a request to regress her hypnotically, I was impressed with her attitude and previous record. To begin with, Mrs. Tuton is the wife of a prominent professional man in her community, and her attitude has been one of cautious observation rather than firm belief from the beginning. "I feel such a strong attachment to the person of Anne Boleyn," she explained to me, "and have from the time I was about eleven or twelve years old. Many features of my own life and circumstances lead me to believe that I either *was* she or was very closely associated with her."

It didn't occur to Mrs. Tuton until recently to put all these so-called clues together, although she has lived with them all her life. Her interest in the subject of reincarnation was aroused by the literature in the field, notably Ruth Montgomery's work. Eventually she read my book *Born Again* and approached me. "At the age of eleven I read a book called *Brief Gaudy Hour* by Margaret Campbell. It concerned the life of Anne Boleyn and her short time as Queen of England. The odd fact is that though I read scores of historical novels and literally hundreds of other books all through childhood and adolescence, majoring eventually in French literature at Wellesley, I never had a feeling—visceral knowledge—to compare with that which I had experienced as a child reading the short life of Anne Boleyn."

From early childhood, Mrs. Tuton had an almost pathological terror of knives and sharp metallic objects, while other weapons did not affect her in the least. The very mention of a blade produced an attack of goose bumps and shivers in her. "I also have frequently experienced a severe sensation of the cutting of a major nerve at the back of my neck, a physical feeling intense enough for me to have consulted a neurosurgeon at the Lahey Clinic about it. No known physiological cause for the sensation could be found, yet it continues to appear from time to time."

Mrs. Tuton also pointed out to me that her given names were Charlotte and Anne, yet from her earliest recollections she had told her mother that Charlotte was the wrong name for her and that she should have been known only as Anne. Her mother had named her Charlotte after her own name but had selected Anne as the second name from an obscure relative, having given the choice of a second name for her child a great deal of thought and finally settling upon one that she considered perfect.

"Another theme has run through my life which is rather twofold," Mrs. Tuton continued her account. "It is a sense of having lost a way of life in high places, among people whose decisions affected the course of history at every turn, and an accompanying sense of having been wrongly accused of some act that I did not commit, or some attitude that I did not hold. None of these feelings can be explained in any way by my present lifetime."

Mrs. Betty Thigpen of South Carolina spent her childhood and adolescence in what she describes as "uneventful middle-class surroundings" and worked for some time as private secretary to a local textile executive. Later she became the personal secretary of a well-known United States senator and eventually managed his South Carolina office. After her marriage to a banking executive, she retired and devoted herself to her children. Mrs. Thigpen's interest in reincarnation is of comparatively recent origin and was prompted by certain events in her own life.

"Since early childhood, I have had certain strong identification feelings with the personality of Anne Boleyn. From the time I was old enough to read, I have also been captivated by sixteenth-century English history," Mrs. Thigpen explained. "I have never been to England but feel strong ties with that country, as well as with France. When I saw the movie, *Anne of the Thousand Days*, sitting almost hypnotized, I felt somehow as if all of it had happened before, but to me. I am almost embarrassed to admit feelings of spiritual kinship with a queen, so I keep telling myself that if there is some connection, perhaps it is just that I knew her, maybe as scullery maid or lady in waiting, but in any event I do feel a definite identification with Anne Boleyn and that period of history that I have never felt with anyone or anything else."

I would like to note that I tried to hypnotize both Mrs. Tuton of Boston and Mrs. Thigpen of South Carolina, but without much success. Both ladies seemed too tense to be able to relax sufficiently to go under to the third stage of hypnosis where regression into a possible previous life might be attempted. Under the circumstances, it is difficult to assess the evidential value of the ladies' statements, but there were far more glamorous and luckier queens to identify with, if this were merely a question of associating oneself with someone desirable. Possibly, as time goes on, these individuals will remember some historical detail that they would not otherwise know, and in this way the question of who they were, if indeed they were, in Queen Anne Boleyn's days may be resolved.

If Anne Boleyn had just cause to be dissatisfied with her sudden death, a relative of hers who also made it to the throne was not so innocent of the charges leveled against her. I am speaking, of course, of Catherine Howard, whom Henry VIII married when he was of advanced years and she was much younger. Catherine took a lover or two and unfortunately was discovered in the process and accused of high treason. She too lost her head. According to the magazine *Country Life,* Hampton Court is the place where she does her meandering, causing all sorts of disturbances as a result. "Such was the fear of an apparition," states Edward

Perry, "that for many years the haunted gallery was shut off. Servants slipped past its doors hastily; the passage outside it is rarely used at night. And still inexplicable screams continue."

No other historical figure has attracted so much identification attention as Mary Queen of Scots, with the possible exception of Cleopatra. This is not surprising, as Mary was a highly controversial figure in her own time. She has been the subject of several plays and numerous books, the best of which is, I believe, Elizabeth Byrd's *Immortal Queen.* Her controversial status is due not so much to an untimely demise at the hands of the executioner, acting on orders from her cousin, Queen Elizabeth I, as to the reasons why Mary was dispatched into eternity in the first place. Nearly all dramatizations and books make a great deal of Queen Elizabeth's hatred and envy of her cousin, and a lot less of the fact that Mary was next in line to the English throne and conspired to get it. While the justice of Mary's imprisonment by Elizabeth may be open to question and could be construed as an act of envy and hatred, Mary's execution, after so many years of imprisonment "in style" in a country castle, is directly traceable to *overt* actions by Mary to remove Elizabeth from the throne. Under the circumstances, and following the rather stern dictates of her time, Elizabeth was at least legally justified in ordering Mary's execution.

Much has also been made in literature of Queen Mary's four ladies in waiting, all first-named Mary as well. They shared her triumphant days at Holyrood Castle in Edinburgh, and they shared her exile in England. "The Four Marys" are reasonably well known to students of history, although these details are not taught on the high school or even average college level in the United States. I think it is important to know the background of what I am about to relate in order to evaluate the relative likelihood of its being true.

In July of 1972 I was approached by Marilyn Smith, a young housewife from St. Louis, Missouri, who had strong reincarnation memories she wished to explore further. At least two of the reincarnation memories, or previous lives, had nothing to do with Scotland, but seemed rather evidential from the details Mrs. Smith was able to communicate to me when we met the following spring in St. Louis. Despite the reincarnation material, Mrs. Smith does not have a strong history of ESP, which is in line with my thinking that true reincarnation memories preclude mediumship. Her involvement with Scottish history began eighteen years before she met me, in 1954.

"When I was seventeen years old, I was curled up in a chair reading and halfway watching television, where a live performance of *Mary Queen of Scots* was being presented. One particular scene caught my attention. In it, Mary, the Queen, is ready to board a boat for an ill-fated journey to England. A woman is clinging to Mary, pleading with her not to go to England. Suddenly I said to myself, 'That woman there, the one who is pleading, is *me*,' but immediately I dismissed this notion. When the queen did get into the boat, I felt a terrible, cowardly guilt."

Mrs. Smith has no Scottish blood in her, has never been to Scotland or England, and has not even read much about it. A few months later she had a vision. "I lived in the country at the time, and because it was a hot summer night, I took my pillow and a blanket and crawled upon a huge wagonload of hay to sleep. I lay there looking up at the beautiful starlit sky, wondering why I hadn't appreciated its beauty before. Then I felt a magnetic force engulf me, and I began predicting the future for myself. 'The stars will play a very important role in my life someday and I'm going to be very rich and famous because of them.' Then I saw the face of a very beautiful blond woman, and somehow I knew she would play an important role in my future. 'We *were* almost like sisters,' I said to myself. But then I caught myself. How could we have been like sisters when I hadn't even met her yet? At this moment I suddenly recalled the television program I had watched with such strange feelings, and the word Mary seemed to be connected with this face. Also, something about a Mary Beaton or Mary Seaton came through, but I didn't understand it."

During the ensuing years, bits and pieces from a previous lifetime seemed to want to come through to the surface, but Mrs. Smith repressed them. Years passed, and Mrs. Smith became interested in the occult, reincarnation, and especially astrology. She began to study astrology and is now erecting horoscopes professionally.

"At my very first astrology lesson," Mrs. Smith explained, "I met another student whose name was Pat Webbe, a very attractive blond woman. There was an almost instant rapport between us. Hers was the face I had seen in my vision many years before, and I decided to tell her of it. However, I didn't inform her of the fact that the name Mary had also been attached to her face, assuming that it had referred to the Blessed Virgin Mary, to whom I was very devoted at all times."

About a year before she met Marilyn Smith, Pat Webbe had a strange dream. In the dream she was dressed in a period gown of several centuries ago. She was in what seemed to be a castle and was waiting to escape.

"It was a large castle and cold, and I remember going into one room, and there were men in it with long halberds who were jabbing at each other. I saw two headgears crushed, and then I was back in the other room and there seemed to be fire everywhere in front of the castle. I hear myself tell a servant to hurry and get the children and make sure they have their coats on, because we have to go out into the snow. I can see the light coming down from where the servant is getting the children, and we go out through a little trap door and there is a large dog out there, but I am not afraid of the dog for some reason, although in my present life I am very much afraid of dogs. The dream ends, but I know at the very end that I am concerned about my oldest daughter not being there."

"Did you see yourself in this dream?" I asked.

"Yes, but it was really just a form; I couldn't distinguish a face or anything."

"What other details do you recall?"

"I recall the period costume and the hooped dresses, but everything was sort of gray, except for the snow and the fire, which was red, and the swords, which were black. I heard thunder, but I can't explain it. But ever since I was a child I have had a recurrent dream. My mother and I were in a boat, and it looked as though we were glad we were in that boat, escaping."

Mrs. Webbe has no strong feeling of having lived before. She has never been to Europe, and she does not have a strong desire to visit Scotland or England, though she does feel she would like to go to France.

"When you met Marilyn Smith for the first time, did you have any peculiar feelings about her, as if you had known her before?" I asked.

"No, but we took up with each other immediately. We were like sisters within six months, almost as if we had been friends all our lives."

Some time after meeting Marilyn Smith, Pat had another unusual dream. In it, she saw herself in bed, and a woman who was supposed to take care of her. Somehow Mrs. Webbe got the name Merrick.

"I remember she had to leave, but I didn't want her to. I begged her to stay, but she had to go anyway. I remember I was sitting at a child-sized piano and playing it beautifully. I could see a great massive door, and a man came in wearing a period costume. It was gray and had some kind of chain belt around it; he had blond hair, and I remember throwing myself at his feet and saying. 'Help her, help her,' and adding, 'She's leaving in a boat, help her,' but he swore and said something about 'Goddamn insurrectionists,' and that was the end of the dream."

"Pat and I often discussed our dreams with each other," Marilyn Smith said. "One day she called me very excitedly about a dream she had just had."

"Well, I thought it was rather silly," Mrs. Webbe explained, "but in the dream my husband and I were at some sort of banquet and we were walking through a long corridor which was very ornately decorated in the French style. There was a couch in one corner with two swords on it. One was very large and ornate, the other small and made of silver, and I handed the latter to my husband. As I handed him the sword, I pricked my finger, and I went to a little room to clean the blood from my hand, and the blood disappeared. When I looked into a mirror in this room, I saw myself dressed as a French boy. Then I said to myself, 'I am Mary Queen of Scots,' and I ran back into the other room and told my husband, 'I am Mary Queen of Scots.' Shortly afterwards I awoke from my dream, singing a song with the words, 'I am Mary Queen of Scots!' "

The two ladies came to the conviction that they had been together in a previous life in Scotland; to be exact, as Mary Queen of Scots and Mary Beaton or Seaton, one of the four ladies in waiting. At first, the idea of having been a Scottish queen was difficult for Pat to accept, and she maintained a healthy attitude of skepticism, leaving the more enthusiastic support of this theory to her friend Marilyn. Nevertheless, the two ladies discussed the matter intelligently and even went so far as to compare horoscopes, since both of them were now immensely interested in astrology. There were a number of incidents into which they read some significance, incidents which taken individually seem to me to have no meaning whatever, but which, taken together in relation to this particular situation, are, at the very least, curious. These include such incidents as

Marilyn Smith visiting a folk theater in Arkansas while on vacation and hearing a folk singer render "The Ballad of Mary Queen of Scots" the minute she arrived. Similarly, there was the time when Pat Webbe attended a floor show in Las Vegas, with one of the principal performers impersonating Mary Queen of Scots.

"I also thought it kind of strange that I never liked the name Mary," Pat Webbe added. "I have five daughters, and my husband had wanted to call our first daughter Mary, but I just wouldn't have it. I wanted something different, but somehow I was compelled to add the name Mary to each one of my daughters somewhere, not because my husband suggested it, but for some unknown reason. So it happened that every one of my daughters has Mary as part of her name."

Since the two ladies, professional astrologers by now, tried to tie in their own rebirth with the horoscope of Mary Queen of Scots and her lady in waiting, they asked that I ascertain the birth data of Mary Beaton and Mary Seaton, if I could. With the help of my friend Elizabeth Byrd, I was able to establish that Mary Queen of Scots was born December 8, 1542, but the inquiry at the Royal Register House supplied only the rather vague information that Mary Seaton seems to have been born around 1541, and there was no reference to the birth of Mary Beaton. Marilyn Smith found it significant that the queen's rising sign had been 29° Taurus, and Pat Webbe, supposed reincarnation of the queen, had a moon in 29° Taurus in her natal chart. She believes that astrology can supply valid information concerning reincarnation identities.

Elizabeth Page Kidder, who lives with her parents near Washington, D.C., happened to be in Scotland at age seven.

"We were on the bus from the airport, going to Edinburgh. Suddenly my father said, 'Look up at the hill; that's where Mary Queen of Scots used to live.' At that, I went into trance, sort of a deep sleep." Somehow her father's reference to Mary Queen of Scots had touched off a buried memory in her. Two days after their arrival in the Scottish capital the Kidders went shopping. While they were looking at kilts, Elizabeth insisted upon getting a Stuart plaid, to the exclusion of all others. In the end, she settled for a MacDonald plaid, which fit in with her family background. A while later, the family went to visit Madame Tussaud's Wax Museum in London. When Elizabeth got a good look at the representation of Mary Queen of Scots being beheaded, she was shattered. Although the seven-year-old girl had never heard of the queen before, she insisted that the execution had been unjust and became extremely vehement about it. None of the other exhibits in the museum affected her in the least. When the family visited Westminster Abbey, Elizabeth went straight to Mary's grave and began to pray for her. Now eighteen years old, Elizabeth Kidder has read a number of books dealing with Mary Queen of Scots, and in particular the references to Mary Seaton have interested her.

Her daughter's strange behavior in Edinburgh and London made Mrs. Kidder wonder about reincarnation and the validity of such incidents. Many years later, when she heard of an organization called The Fellowship of Universal Guidance in Los Angeles, specializing in life studies along the lines of Edgar Cayce's work, she submitted the necessary data to them for a reading concerning her daughter. Did her daughter have any connection with Mary Queen of Scots, she wanted to know. Back came the answer that she had been her lady in waiting. Mrs. Kidder went further, accepting the so-called life reading at face value, and began to put her daughter into hypnosis, finding her a good subject. Under hypnosis Elizabeth disclosed further details of her life as lady in waiting to Mary Queen of Scots and claimed that her school friend Carol was, in fact, Mary Queen of Scots reincarnated. Carol Bryan William, who had come along to visit me in New York, had often dreamed that she was a richly dressed person standing in an ornately carved room with royal-blue hangings. Bent on proving the truth of these amazing claims, Mrs. Kidder contacted Ruth Montgomery and, in her own words, "was able to verify through her that her daughter Elizabeth was Mary Seaton and her friend Carol was Mary Queen of Scots."

Carol, who is a little older than Elizabeth, said that when she was little she always thought that she was from England. Her father is of English descent, but since she is an adopted child, that would have little meaning in this instance. She does have recurrent dreams involving a castle and a certain room in it, as well as a countryside she likes to identify as English.

I had previously put Elizabeth under hypnosis, but without significant results. I next tried my hand with Carol. She turned out to be a better subject, sliding down to the third level easily. I asked her to identify the place she was now in.

"I think it is the sixteenth century. I see lots of

townspeople. They are dressed in burlap, loose-fitting cloth gathered in by a rope around the waist. I see myself standing there, but it is not me. I am a boy. He is small, has fair hair, and is kind of dirty."

On further prodding, it turned out that the boy's name was John, that his mother was a seamstress and his father a carpenter, working for the king. The king's name was James. He had dark hair and a beard and was on the tall side.

"Do you know anyone else in the city?" I asked.

"I know a woman. People don't like her very much because she is not Catholic. She is Episcopal."

"What are you?"

"Catholic."

"Is everybody Catholic in your town?"

"Some people aren't, but if you are not, you are in trouble. It is the law."

"Who is the man who leads the ones who are not Catholic?"

"Henry VIII."

"Does he like King James?"

"I don't think so."

"What happened to King James?"

"He is killed. He died a violent death."

"Did Henry VIII have anything to do with it?"

"There was a discrepancy over the religions. Henry VIII did not want to be Catholic, and the only way he could abolish Catholic rule was to get rid of James."

"Who wins?"

"I think Henry VIII does, but he does and he doesn't. Everybody does not follow Henry VIII. There are still people who are faithful to the Catholic religion."

After I returned Carol to the conscious state, I questioned her about her studies. It turned out she was taking an English course at college and had had one year of English history thus far. She had no particular interest in Scottish history, but she seemed unusually attached to the subject of the Catholic religion. She can't understand why, because she is an Episcopalian.

Mrs. Kidder wasn't too pleased that her protégée, Carol, remembered only having been a boy in sixteenth-century England, and not the eminent Mary Queen of Scots. But then where would that leave Pat Webbe of St. Louis? It was all just as well.

Linda Wise is a young lady living in the Midwest whose ancestors came over on the *Mayflower*. She is part Scottish, part English and part German, and just about her only link with Scotland is a family legend from her grandmother's side that several members of the family were forced to leave Scotland in the 1700's on very short notice. These cousins, if they were that, were named Ewing, but Miss Wise hasn't researched it further. She has never had any particular interest in Scotland or Great Britain, hasn't studied the history of the British Isles, and, living in the Midwest, has very little contact with English or Scottish people. Nevertheless, she has had periodic feelings of wanting to *go back to* Scotland, as if she had been there before. In 1971 she became acquainted with a Scottish couple and they became pen pals. As a result, she went to visit them in

August, 1972. As soon as she arrived in Scotland, she had a strange experience.

"When I first got there, we took a bus from Aberdeen to Elgin, where my friends live. I could see the mountains in a certain area and suddenly I had goose bumps. I just felt as if I had come home, as if I had known the area from before."

Later she went to visit England, but all the time she was in England she felt extremely uneasy, wanting to return to Scotland as soon as possible. "For some reason, I felt much safer once the train crossed the border at Berwick-on-Tweed."

But the most haunting experience of her journey took place at the battleground of Culloden, where Bonnie Prince Charlie led the Scottish clans against King George in the Uprising of 1745. This battlefield, situated several miles east of Inverness, is now a historical site. Miss Wise had a vague knowledge that an important battle had taken place at Culloden, and that it had been extremely bloody. The forest at Culloden contains many grave markers, and people go there to observe and sometimes pray.

"Suddenly I felt as if I were being pulled in two directions—to continue and yet to get back to the main road as fast as I could," Linda Wise explained to me. "At a certain point I could not take it any longer, so I left to rejoin the friends I had come with. They too commented on the eerie sensations they were having."

"What exactly did you feel at Culloden?"

"I felt that something or someone was after me, that I wasn't alone," Miss Wise explained. "I really didn't feel as if I were by myself." When Miss Wise rejoined her friends, she took with her some small stones from the area. On returning to the Midwest, she handed a small stone from Culloden to her mother to use in an attempt at psychometry. Immediately Mrs. Wise picked up the impression of a group of men, wearing predominantly red and yellow uniforms, coming over a hill. This experiment was part of a regular session undertaken by a home development circle among people interested in psychic research.

"We asked my mother to describe the uniform she was impressed with," Miss Wise continued. "She said Scottish; she did not see any kilts or straight-legged pants, however. She physically felt her own eyes becoming very heavy as if they were being pushed in. Since my mother knew that there was nothing wrong with her own eyes, she mentally asked what was the cause of it and in her mind's eye saw a form, or rather the etheric image of a large man who said he wanted his eyeballs back! He explained that he had been hanging around for a long time for that reason and did not know what to do."

"You mean, he had lost his eyes?"

"Yes," Linda confirmed. "My mother realized that this was an emotional situation, so she calmed his fears and told him his eyes were well again and to go on, sending him love, energy and assurance at the same time."

Some time after her return to the United States, Miss Wise bought a record on which the famous Black Watch Regiment was playing. It upset her greatly, but her emotional involvement became even stronger when she went to a midwestern festival where various ethnic groups participated. "It was the first pipe band I had seen since I had been to Scotland, and I got tears in my eyes and felt like being back in Scotland."

The battle of Culloden, and the fate of Bonnie Prince Charlie, at one time King Charles III of Scotland and England, has also affected my own life for many years, because of some as yet indistinct memories of having lived during that time. People have given me objects from Culloden, or concerning Prince Charles; books, sometimes of very obscure origin, have found their way into my hands. Moreover, I own a silver touch piece with the name of Charles III, a great rarity as medals go, acquired under strange circumstances. At the time I saw it listed in the catalogue of a well-known London art dealer, the catalogue had been on its way to me for some time, having been sent by sea mail. Nevertheless, undaunted, I sent away for the piece but had very little hope that the modestly priced touch piece would still be there. Picture my surprise when I was nevertheless able to acquire it. How the many Scottish collectors of such items passed over this most desirable medal, so that it could await my letter, seems to me beyond pure chance or logic. It was almost as if the medal were *meant* to be mine.

4·

LONGLEAT'S GHOSTS

Longleat in Somerset must be the most publicized haunted house in all of England. If it isn't, at the very least its owner, Lord Bath, is the most publicity-conscious man among British nobility I have ever met: a genial, clever, very businesslike Aquarian who happens to share my birthdate, although a few years my senior. Longleat and its ghosts were first extensively publicized by Tom Corbett, the British society seer, who went there in the company of a British journalist, Diana Norman, who then wrote a book on Corbett's experiences in various British houses called *The Stately Ghosts of England*. Mr. Corbett goes to great pains to explain that he is not a medium but a clairvoyant. He most certainly is not a trance medium, and it takes a good deep-trance medium to really get to the bottom of any haunting. All a clairvoyant can do is pick up

vibrations from the past and possibly come into communication with a resident ghost or spirit entity, while
it remains for a trance medium to allow the spirit or
ghost to speak directly to the investigator.

I began to correspond with Lord Bath in the spring
of 1964, but before I could fix a date for my first visit to
Longleat, NBC television decided to include the magnificent palace in its itinerary of allegedly haunted
houses which its documentary unit wanted to film.

The *Psychic News* of May 23, 1964, headlined, FA-
MOUS ACTRESS AND MEDIUM TO STAR IN PSYCHIC FILM
—WILL CAMERA RECORD SPIRIT FORMS? The newspaper was, of course, referring to Margaret Rutherford,
the grand old lady of the British theater, who happened
to be interested in ESP phenomena, although by no
means a medium herself.

The idea of filming at Longleat and elsewhere was
the brainchild of producer-director Frank De Fellitta,
who had read the Tom Corbett–Diana Norman tome
on Britain's haunted mansions. The NBC team went to
Longleat, and immediately after they had set up for the
filming all sorts of difficulties arose. Cameras would be
out of place, tools would disappear; it seemed as if the
resident ghosts were not altogether happy at the invasion taking place. But it is hard to tell how much of the
reported difficulty was factual and how much of it a
product of the NBC publicity department. One fact,
however, was blissfully ignored in its implications by
both NBC and the producer. They had set up a time-
lapse exposure camera in the haunted corridor at Longleat, a camera which records one frame of film at a time

over a long period of time. Such a recording was made during the night when no one was around. On developing the film, a whitish flash of light was discovered for which there was no easy explanation. The flash of light could not be explained as faulty film, faulty laboratory work, or any other logical source. What the camera had recorded was nothing less than the formation of a spirit form. Had Mr. De Fellitta any basic knowledge of parapsychology or had he been in the company of an expert in the field, he might have made better use of this unexpected bonus.

The choice of Margaret Rutherford as hostess of the program was not dictated by psychic ability or her integrity as an investigator, but simply because she looked the part, and in television that is the most important consideration. And she had played the magnificently written comedy role of the medium in Noel Coward's *Blithe Spirit*. Even the austere *New York Times*, which has generally ignored any serious treatment of parapsychology, managed to give the project and Margaret Rutherford quite a bit of space. "Miss Rutherford and company will visit allegedly spirit-ridden mansions. She will give her personal impressions of the hauntings —how they occur, when they occur and, maybe, why they don't occur," wrote Paul Gardner. Nothing of the sort was either intended or delivered, of course, but it read well in the publicity releases.

My first visit to Longleat took place in September, 1964, long after the hullabaloo and the departure of Margaret Rutherford and the film crew. However, the usual large number of tourists was still milling around, so we had arranged with Lord Bath to come at a time when the grounds were closed to them.

Longleat is in the west of England, about three hours from London by car, and truly a palace, rivaling some of the royal residences in both size and appointments. Lord Bath himself had long ago moved into more modest quarters at nearby Warminster, where he and his wife lived in a charming old mill. Longleat itself is named after a river which runs through the grounds. It has been the home of the Thynne family for four hundred years. Sometime before 1580 Sir John Thynne, direct ancestor of the current Marquess of Bath, began to build Longleat. His successors enlarged the mansion until it assumed the proportions of a palace. To describe the art treasures that fill the palace from top to bottom would take volumes. Suffice it to say that some very important paintings hang at Longleat and among them, perhaps a peculiarity of the present Lord Bath, art work by both Sir Winston Churchill and Adolf Hitler. The latter are in the private portion of the house, however, on one of the upper floors.

The first person Lord Bath wanted us to meet was the old nurse, a certain Miss Marks, who was then in her seventies. At the time when she took care of little Caroline, she had several encounters with a ghost.

"I saw a tall, scholarly looking man," the nurse explained. "He was walking along and looked as if he might be reading something; I only saw his back, but he had a high collar, the wings of it distinctly standing out. I would say, 'I think perhaps that is Grandpa. Shall we hurry up and speak to him?' We would follow him across the room, but when we got to the door at the end, which was shut, he just wasn't there. I didn't think anything of it, because I saw him lots and lots of times, and in the end I thought, It isn't a person at all. I didn't discuss it with anyone, but I knew it was friendly to me. I loved seeing this person, even after I discovered it was *only a ghost.*"

From the nurse's description and that given by Tom Corbett it was clear to historians that the ghost was none other than the builder of Longleat, Sir John Thynne. Thynne had been a banker in the time of Henry VIII and was known for his sharp business sense. The grounds upon which Longleat stands were a result of his business acumen, and he was very much attached to it in his day. His haunting ground, so to speak, is the Red Library on the ground floor, where he usually appears between seven and eight o'clock at night.

Lord Bath then took us up to the haunted corridor, which is now completely bare and gives a rather depressing feeling, ghost or no ghost. This long, narrow passage runs parallel to the sleeping quarters of some of the Thynne family, and it was here that Tom Corbett felt a ghostly presence.

"This is the corridor," Lord Bath explained in a voice that betrayed the fact that he had said it many times before, "where a duel was fought by one of my ancestors, the second Viscount Weymouth, because he found that his wife, Louisa Carteret, had been unfaithful to him. He discovered her in a state, unfortunately, in which he thought a duel ought to be fought with the man she was with. He fought this duel with the intruder and killed the man, after which he buried him in the cellar. His skeleton was accidentally found when the boiler was put in downstairs six years ago."

One would assume the unfortunate lover to be roaming the corridors at Longleat, seeking revenge, or at least, to frighten the survivors. But apparently he took his fate like a man and remained a spirit rather than a ghost. Not so with Lady Louisa: "People have seen what is assumed to be the ghost of Louisa Carteret," Lord Bath explained. "I haven't seen her myself, because I don't have that power. My mother has seen the ghost in the Red Library downstairs, but not this one." I asked about visitors. Lord Bath explained that visitors were never taken to the part of the house where we were, so there was no way of telling whether they had experienced anything. I took a good look at the portrait of Lady Louisa. She was indeed worth fighting over: lovely face, beautiful eyes, slim figure in a green dress.

Shortly afterwards we left Longleat with the firm promise to return someday with a trance medium so that we could have a go at contacting the resident ghosts. But it wasn't until two years later that the opportunity came along.

It was in September, 1966, when I brought the London medium and former nurse, Trixie Allingham, to Longleat, introduced her to Lord Bath, and proceeded to enter the palace in the hope of really coming to grips with the phantoms that had never been dislodged, nor indeed fully contacted before. For the next two hours, Lord Bath, my friends and I went through one of the most fascinating and gripping sessions we'd ever experienced.

All along, Trixie, a frail lady, had been unhappy in the car, partly because it was a rough ride and partly because she sensed some great tragedy ahead which would shortly involve her personally. As we were rounding the last long curve of the driveway leading to the palace, Trixie turned to me and said, "I saw the painting of a fair young woman. I thought she had something to do with my visit here, and she showed me an opened window as if she were telling me that there had been a tragedy connected with that window. Either she was pushed out, or somebody she loved had flung himself out, and then the vision faded. Then another woman came to me, rather charming and of the same period. She was older and looked rather haughty for a moment. Then she faded."

I had not replied, for I did not wish to give her any clues. A few minutes later we arrived at the main gate to Longleat and got out of the car. I gave Trixie time to "get to herself" and to get the shaky ride out of her system. Then we entered the Red Library, and I asked Trixie to sit down in one of the large antique chairs at the head of the room.

Immediately she said in a quivering, excited voice, "A long time ago something very evil happened here, or someone had a devilish temptation in this room, looking out of that window." She pointed at one of the several large windows on the far side of the room. "I have a feeling that there is a French link here, that either the wife or the daughter was of French ancestry," Trixie continued. "There is some connection with the French Revolution, for I see a guillotine . . . good heavens!"

"Do you sense a ghost here, Trixie?" I asked.

"As a matter of fact, yes, I get a woman. She has a dress with long sleeves, and she walks as if her hip were bent. There is a crucifix around her neck and she's saying, 'Help me, help me, help me!' This is going back more than a hundred years; her gown is sort of whitish with a mulberry shade. From way back." Trixie paused for a moment as if getting her bearings. Lord Bath, not exactly a believer, was watching her seriously now.

"Now I see a horse and a man galloping away, and I see the woman in tears and I wonder what it means. She sees the man galloping away, and she thinks life is over, and now I see her dead. I feel there is a church nearby, where her effigy is in stone on top of some sort of a sarcophagus. She showed it to me."

I asked Trixie if the woman was the same one she had seen in the car driving up, but she couldn't be sure, for she hadn't yet seen the woman's face. Were there any other presences in the room?

"Yes," Trixie replied. "Very dimly over there by the door and holding the handle, there is a man with a big hat on, and he wears a collar around the neck. He goes back a long time, I think."

I glanced at Lord Bath: nobody had told Trixie about the apparition seen by the nurse—Sir John Thynne, a man wearing a strange old-fashioned collar! While Trixie was resting for a moment, I walked around the library. I noticed that the shelves were filled with French books and that some of the furniture was obviously of eighteenth-century French origin. Had Trixie simply picked up the atmosphere of the room?

Trixie suddenly said in a rather challenging tone of

voice: "Henry—is there a Henry here?" Almost like an obedient schoolboy, Lord Bath stepped forward. Trixie eyed him suspiciously. "You're Henry?"

"I'm the only one."

"Well, they said, 'Go talk to Henry.' "

"Who told you to talk to Henry?" Lord Bath inquired.

"I don't know. It is a man, a very unhappy man. He passed over a long time ago. He killed three people, and I don't mean in battle."

The story was getting more interesting. "How did he kill them?" I demanded to know.

"I look at his hands, and there are brown stains on them which he can't seem to wipe off. The letter H seems to be connected with him, and I have the feeling he did it in vengeance. I see a friar come up to him, and him trying to get absolved and being unable to. The friar is haughty, arrogant, and then the prior comes in and I see this unhappy man on his knees, and yet he does not get absolution, and that is why he comes back here."

"Can you possibly speak to him, Trixie?" I asked.

"I am speaking to him *now*," Trixie replied impatiently, "but he says, 'There is no hope for me.' I tell him we will pray for him. I hear him speak in Latin. I know a fair amount of Latin, and I'm saying it in English: 'Out of the depths I have called unto thee, O God, hear my voice.' Then the monk reappears, and there is also a tall lady here, by his side. I believe this is his wife; she's very slender and beautiful, and she's holding up one of his hands, saying, 'Pray, pray as you've never prayed before.' "

We left the Red Library and slowly walked up the staircase, one of the world's greatest, to the upper stories. When we arrived at the haunted corridor where the famous duel had taken place, Trixie sensed that something had happened around December or January of one particular year—not an ordinary passing. Immediately she explained that it had nothing to do with the haunting downstairs.

"The passing of this person was kept quiet. He was carried out in the dead of night in a gray shroud. I can see this happening. Five people are carrying out this ominous task. The whole situation was tragic and hushed up. He wasn't murdered and it wasn't suicide, but it was a person who came to an untimely end. Above all, they wanted no attention, no attention. He didn't live here, but he stayed here for a while. He came from Spain. I think he died from a wound in his side, yet it wasn't murder or suicide. He was about thirty-five years old. He says 'O my God, my God, to come to such an end.' He was a Catholic, he tells me. He was not shriven here after he passed. I see lanterns; he's not buried in sacred ground. Wait a moment, sir," Trixie suddenly said, turning to Lord Bath. "Is there a name like Winnie or something like that connected with your family?" Lord Bath's interest perked up. Winnie sounded a little like Weymouth.

"Francis, Francis," Trixie said excitedly now. "And I hear the name Fanny. She's just laughing. Did you know her?"

"Yes," Lord Bath replied, "a long, long time ago."

"Was she a very bright person?"

"Well, she was as a child. Her nickname was Fanny."

Evidently Trixie had gotten some more recent spirits mixed in with the old characters. "I see her as a younger woman, lovely, laughing, running along, and she tells me you have in your pocket a coin that is bent, out of order, not a normal coin. Is that true?"

"Yes," Lord Bath said, surprised.

"She just told me; isn't she sweet? Oh, and there is a lord chief justice here. Do you know him?"

"Peculiar," Lord Bath replied. "There *was* a lord chief justice upstairs."

For a moment Trixie seemed particularly sad, as she reported: "There is a child here named Tim, Timothy, but he died at the age of one and a half. If this true?"

Lord Bath seemed to struggle with his emotions now. "Yes," he finally said in a low voice.

"He wants me to say, 'I am Tim,' and you should know he is still your son."

Lord Bath confirmed that his oldest son, Tim, had died in infancy, but that the fact was known only to members of the family and had never been publicized.

Trixie then reported a servant woman, continuing to serve in her ghostly condition, and when I didn't show any particular interest, she went on to say that there was also a rather funny-looking man, "someone holding his head under his arm, walking, and I really shouldn't laugh at this sort of thing, but I saw this man with his head under his arm."

Since none of us were laughing, she assumed that it was all right to address the man with his head under his arm. "Can you tell me, sir, how you lost your head, and why?" She listened for a while, apparently getting an answer from the unseen headless specter. Nodding, she turned to us. "There is something about some rebels here; they are linked with France, and these rebels have come in strength. Somebody was being hounded, a person of high birth. He was hidden here, and I don't like it at all."

Lord Bath was visibly impressed. "During the rebellion of the Duke of Monmouth," he explained, "some rebels took refuge here. It is not at all unlikely that one of them was put to death on these grounds."

Trixie now exhibited unmistakable signs of weariness. Under the circumstances, we decided to call it a day and return in the morning. The following morning we started again in the Red Library. On entering, Trixie described a woman walking up and down wringing her hands and saying that her child had died. Trixie identified her as Christina and explained that this had happened no more than a hundred years ago. However, my main interest was in an earlier period, and I asked Trixie to try for full trance if she could. Again she seated herself in the comfortable chair at the far end of the Red Library.

"There is a link here with the tragedy I saw in part yesterday," she began. "I still see the horseman and the woman at the window, and I smell the tragedy. There is something about a rapier wound. Ron is murdered and a Helen is mixed up in this. The man I saw yesterday is still here, by the way, and he looks happier now."

"Ask him to identify himself."

"I get the initial R. He wears a cape and a lace collar."

"Why did he murder the three people?"

"I get the initial P. Someone was in a dungeon

here." All of a sudden we weren't hearing Trixie's voice anymore, but a rough male voice coming from her entranced lips. I realized that the ghost had at last taken over the medium and was about to address us directly.

"Who put you into the dungeon?"

"S. Mine enemy, mine enemy."

"Is this your house?"

"Yes, of course."

"Did you build this house?"

"With bad money."

"What is your name, sir?" I insisted.

Suddenly the entity was gone again and Trixie was back. "He was a Catholic by birth," she said, "and he is showing me a very large ruby ring on his finger. His ankles hurt him. He must have been chained for a time, and I see a short dagger in his hand. Now he is fading again."

"Is he the victim or the murderer?" I almost shouted.

"He did it; he says, 'I did it, I have no peace.' He was the owner of the house. He says, 'You will pray for me, you will pray for me.' " I assured the entity through the medium that we would all pray for him.

"He says someone owes him something."

"But he can be forgiven; tell him that."

"There is a little chapel here somewhere in this mansion. I can see the altar, and he wants Lord Bath to go there, to the chapel. 'If he will do it, he will give me peace; he will give me rest.' "

I promised that we would do it, without even asking Lord Bath, for I knew he would go along with it, although he was not a religious person.

"I can't do any more, I can't do any more," the medium said now, and she looked exhausted. I questioned her about what she remembered.

"I saw two men killed over a woman," Trixie recollected. "There is a lead coffin amongst all the others, one different from the others. It is away from the others. This man is in it, the one who murdered. I hear the name Grace, and someone was hung, hanged from the rafters."

Impressions seemed to hit her now from various directions, possibly getting different layers of history confused in the process. It was up to us to sort it out.

"Tom," Trixie now said firmly, and looked at me. I asked her to describe the man. "I see him very dimly; he is old and belongs to an earlier age." Lord Bath then informed me that we were in what used to be the chapel, although the floor had been changed and we were actually above it. Just as I had promised, we grouped ourselves around the spot where the altar once stood below, bowed our heads in prayer, and I said, "May Thomas rest free from worry, happy in his home. May he be free from any guilt or fear. Let us now have a moment of silent prayer."

In the silence I glanced at Lord Bath, a man who had told me before that he thought himself an agnostic. He seemed genuinely affected and moved.

"I don't know whether it was a bishop," Trixie said, "but I saw a man with a gold miter on his head make the sign of the cross and I heard the word 'progression,' and then something very odd happened. A feather was put on his shoulder, but I don't know what it means."

"Perhaps his soul is now light as a feather?" I suggested. Trixie then asked Lord Bath whether he knew of any jeweled crucifix in the mansion. Lord Bath could not remember such an item offhand. Trixie insisted, "It is a jeweled cross with dark stones, and it has to do with your people. I also see three monks who were here when you were praying. Three in a row. But now I feel peace; I feel a man who had a leaden weight on his shoulder is now without it. It was important that he be helped."

I have already mentioned that the name which the medium got in connection with the death of the thirty-five-year-old Spaniard in the haunted passage upstairs sounded very close to Weymouth, the man who killed him in a duel. The medium's description of this man's death as being neither death nor suicide is of course entirely correct: he was killed in an honest duel, which in those days was not considered murder. Trixie described the man's death as an affair that had to be hushed up, and so it was indeed, not only because a man had been killed, but also because the wife of the viscount had been unfaithful. A scandal *was* avoided: the body was interred underneath the kitchen floor, and, as Lord Bath confirmed, it had been found several years earlier and been given burial *outside* the house.

More fascinating is Trixie's account of the haunting in the Red Library. The man she described is obviously the same man described by the old nanny whom I interviewed in 1964, and the same man whom Dorothy Coates, former librarian of Longleat, had encountered, as well as a certain Mrs. Grant, former housekeeper in the greathouse.

In a somewhat confused and jumbled way, however, Trixie hit on many of the facts surrounding the ancient palace. I doubt that Trixie would have known of these family secrets, which are never found in tourist guides of Longleat or in popular books dealing with the Thynne family. They are, however, available in research libraries, if one tries hard enough to find the information. There exists, for instance, a contemporary source known as the "John Evelyn Diary," a seventeenth-century chronicle of the London scene. From this source we learned that Thomas Thynne, then already one of the wealthiest men in England and somewhat advanced in years, had fallen in love with a sixteen-year-old heiress by the name of Elizabeth Ogle. He married her despite the great difference in their ages, and after the wedding ceremony preceded her to Longleat, where Lady Elizabeth was to follow him in a few days' time. But Elizabeth never arrived in Longleat. Unwilling to consummate the marriage into which she felt herself forced by her family, she ran away to the Netherlands, where she continued living as if she weren't married. In the Netherlands, Elizabeth Ogle met a certain Count Koenigsmark and fell in love with this somewhat adventurous gentleman. Since divorce was out of the question, and Lady Elizabeth was legally married to Thomas Thynne, the young lovers decided to murder Elizabeth's husband so that she might be free to marry her count.

In view of Thynne's affluence and importance, such a plot was not an easy one to bring off. Koenigsmark therefore engaged the services of three paid murderers, a certain Lieutenant Stern, a Colonel Vratz and a man named Boroski. The murderous foursome arrived in London and immediately set about keeping a close watch on their intended victim. One Sunday night Thynne left a party in London and entered his coach to be driven home. That was the signal they had been waiting for. They followed their victim, and when the coach with Thomas Thynne reached Pall Mall, which was at that time still a country road, the murderers stopped it. Lieutenant Stern, galloping ahead of the coach, put his hands onto the reins of the lead horse. As Thomas Thynne opened the door of the coach and stepped out, a volley of shots hit him in the face.

The restless ghost had called "mine enemy." Could this have been Stern?

The murder created a great deal of attention even in those unruly times. Count Koenigsmark and his henchmen were apprehended just as the count was about to leave England to join Elizabeth. According to John Evelyn, the trial, which took place in 1682, saw the count acquitted by a corrupt jury, but the actual murderers were condemned to death on the gallows. The hired assassins paid with their lives, but the man who had hatched the plot got off scot-free. No wonder the restless spirit of the victim could not find peace! But if one of the ghosts who contacted us through Trixie was indeed Thomas Thynne, the victim of the murder plot, why should he then grieve for the three people who had been put to death for his murder? Undoubtedly, Trixie, in reaching several levels of hauntings, had brought up bits and pieces of John, Thomas, and perhaps even his murderers—all presented in a slightly confusing but essentially evidential package.

Trixie also spoke of "one lead coffin, different from

all others." According to the diaries, two weeks after Colonel Vratz had been put to death his body was still not decayed, owing to a new process of preservation which was being used for the first time. "He lay exposed in a very rich coffin lined with *lead,* too magnificent for so daring and horrid a murderer."

So it seems that at least four ghosts occupied the halls of Longleat: the Lady Louisa, who mourned her lover's death at the hands of her husband; the rebel from the Duke of Monmouth's army, who was caught and slaughtered; the builder of Longleat, Sir John Thynne, whose personal attachment and possibly feelings of guilt keep him from leaving his rich estate for greener pastures; and, of course, Thomas Thynne. I should think the latter has departed the premises now, but I am equally sure that Sir John is still around enjoying the spectacles his descendant, the present Lord Bath, is putting on for the tourists. Surely Sir John would have understood the need to install turnstiles in the cafeteria and toilet downstairs, or to bring in lions for a zoo, and to do whatever was possible to raise revenue to keep the magnificent palace in prime condition; for Sir John, not unlike his descendant, was foremost a man of business and common sense.

5

THE COUNTRYSIDE IS
FULL OF HAUNTINGS

Margaret Rutherford and her husband Stringer
Davis will be delighted to have lunch with us here on
Monday," the note from Ruth Plant read, inviting my
wife and me to visit at her cottage in the woods, The
Crippetts, at Jordans, near Beaconsfield. Ruth and I had
been friends for many years, and she had wanted us to
visit her home on previous occasions. This time the
opportunity was a double one: to meet the celebrated
actress and to talk to a certain Mrs. Beresford, who had
had some extraordinary experiences with ghosts and
apparitions. I could not very well resist such a double
parlay, and so we arrived at Ruth's house in the woods
just a little before one on a sunny September Monday
in 1967. The house contains two stories and a large
veranda, somewhat sloping toward the front, and is
completely surrounded by a lovely garden and tall

trees. Ruth had laid on a superb cold luncheon, and as soon as we stepped inside the house we saw that the two distinguished guests had already arrived. Immediately I went over to introduce myself to Magaret Rutherford and her husband. It turned out that Miss Rutherford was not the least bit interested in discussing psychic phenomena and hadn't the foggiest notion who I was. But a pleasant table conversation ensued nevertheless, and then I excused myself and went to meet Mrs. Vivian Beresford, the psychic lady who lives upstairs. A smallish woman in her later middle years, Mrs. Beresford turned out to be polite and a bit shy, but willing to tell me all about her experiences so that the world might know about them. She had kept a diary of the more amazing incidents and went over it with me.

Sunday, September 4, 1966. "Almost exactly twelve noon, while washing dishes, I turned to get a plate and was surprised to see a man standing in my doorway. As I gazed at him, he appeared to merge with the air, and all I could really see was a pale face and vivid blue eyes. By the position of his head I would say he was fairly tall, but suddenly he was gone. I was so startled, I dropped the plate. I felt shaky and rather sick for a few minutes."

Tuesday, September 6, 1966. "At about two-thirty in the afternoon the same man, that is, just the upper half of him, with hair parted on the side and brushed up and back, appeared to me. This time I was not frightened, but as he dissolved, I again felt sick and weak."

Saturday, September 10, 1966. "At exactly five o'clock, the fair-haired man appeared in the hall of my flat again, only the upper half of him; his hands were visible, and he fingered a ring on his left little finger. He seemed about thirty-five to forty years old. There was a queer disturbance in the air, not a noise. I think he had a tie pin, but my attentions were drawn to his beautiful hands, though I could not see the ring clearly."

Monday, September 12, 1966. "At quarter to two, I became conscious of a disturbance and saw the figure in my sitting room, almost complete this time, with a darkish coat, rather wide, and a small tie pin. I observed his long features, slim build, and a signet ring on his little finger. He smiled. I too smiled, and then he disappeared. These visits exhaust me and cause nausea, but I am *not* frightened."

Wednesday, September 14, 1966. "Another visit from the charming, fair-haired gentleman. This time I spoke to him, asking his name. He made an effort to answer and I faintly heard George. He was nearly complete except for his feet, and he was again twisting his ring as though it had a significance."

Friday, September 16, 1966. "Just as the radio program news ended at seven-fifteen this evening, I saw 'George' on the landing in the flat. For the first time I saw him move, but because his legs were not visible, he gave the odd impression of gliding. I retreated into the kitchen and he stopped in the doorway. I saw his tie pin plainly; it was small and round with a rim of gold and a darkish stone in the center. His ring was also apparent, a colored bezel, and around it was a crest, but I could not make out the crest. His moving rather startled me. I stupidly said, 'Good evening,' at which he smiled. He had on what seemed to be a smoking jacket, and then he started to fade, and the awful exhaustion I suffer on these occasions caused me to say, 'Why me?' and he smiled again. This time I felt really ill, very sick for about fifteen minutes, then I was suddenly all right again."

Wednesday, September 21, 1966. "It was three thirty and I was sitting in my room, sewing. I became conscious of an odd disturbance, and I looked up to see the same fair man standing at the table, looking not at me but at the parrot, who seemed in some strange way aware of him also, for he climbed about the cage, muttering, and then yapped like a dog, as if he were showing off to the ghost. George then turned his head and disappeared."

Friday, September 23, 1966. "Again I saw my fair-haired visitor in the kitchen. This time he was entire and solid—I could not see the window through him. He was visible for two or three minutes, then he faded. Once more I found my strength going and sat down, but it was quickly over."

On July 29, 1967, Mrs. Beresford went over her notes again and put them in order. "I have never seen the fair man again," she concluded her observations on this particular haunt.

When I discussed Mrs. Beresford's extraordinary visitor with Ruth Plant, Ruth explained that she knew very well who the man was. "This man is Sir James Stuart-Menleth," Ruth said, "the father-in-law of Lady Stuart-Menleth, a good friend of mine. He lost a much-prized piece of jewelry in my garden and may still be looking for it: the ring he kept showing Mrs. Beresford, which was a family ring. One night when Sir James went to bed, Lady Stuart-Menleth, my friend, spoke to him, asking him to leave the ring to her eldest son, if he should die. Sir James died that very night in his sleep. When he came to be buried, the ring could not be found!"

Mrs. Beresford thought that the man would never appear again, since his message had been understood. "I think he was pleased that I wasn't frightened," she remarked, "but the awful part was the dreadful exhaustion and nausea occurring every time he appeared. It was as though an elastic band stretched unbearably from me until somehow it broke, like a pulling away of a life force; suddenly it returns and I'm all right again. I can't understand this; the room was full of sunshine, yet he looked solid and real until the fading happened. Why this should happen to me, who has so dreaded ever seeing such things as ghosts, is puzzling, but still more so is the fact that I'm not frightened, nor do I seem to be mad. I sleep well; my appetite is normal. Incidentally, I understand why the parrot recognized my ghostly visitor: Jacko used to belong to Lady Stuart-Menleth, and I was looking after him for her."

"Was that the only time you had a ghostly visitation?" I asked.

Mrs. Beresford shook her head. "A strange thing happened to me last July. Miss Plant had gone to London for a couple of days, and a friend, Mrs. Marshall, was staying with me. That afternoon, she and I were out in the garden, in front, when my attention was drawn to a young man coming in the big gateway. I called out to him, and he asked, 'Is Ruth in?' I said no, she would be away until the next day. He turned to go, so I said,

'Is there a message?' He hesitated, then said, 'It doesn't matter,' but I insisted, 'Well, then, just leave your name so I can tell her who called.' He then said, 'Tell her Richard was passing through.' I turned my head away for an instant, and when I looked back he had disappeared. A neighbor, Mrs. Hogard, had also heard the man's voice and inquired who it was. So I didn't just imagine it."

When Ruth Plant returned she tried to puzzle out who the visitor was, for offhand she could not remember a Richard. It left her no peace, so she went to sit with a reputable medium at Oxford to see whether she might get some clues concerning the strange visitor. It turned out that that very medium had canceled an appointment with a young sitter because of the pressure of work. The young man had left her and had had a fatal automobile accident on the road—close to Ruth Plant's house! The medium obtained a snapshot of the young man in question, and Ruth Plant showed it to Mrs. Beresford, who immediately recognized the young man as her strange caller of that afternoon. Her friend Mrs. Marshall also confirmed that it was a photograph of the visitor. Richard was indeed, as he put it, passing through.

"Extraordinary," I said after we had gone over these experiences in her diary. "Do you still have visitations of this type?"

Mrs. Beresford nodded. "I've been seeing brilliant flashes of light from time to time lately. Miss Plant thought it might be passing cars, but my curtains were tightly drawn on the side that looks out onto the top of the lane, and the other window faces a cupboard with a roof window to give light. Last week I was finding it difficult to sleep in the early hours Sunday morning and had just become pleasantly sleepy when a brilliant light flashed around the room below the windows. It passed over my face and felt like an icy breeze. I then was touched on my arm. I thought it was the cat, only to discover him asleep in his box. Again I tried to go to sleep, and, lying on my back, I was gazing at a luminous spot above my head, rather like the dying bulb in a torch. At the same time an indistinct voice was whispering close to my ear. I could not distinguish any words. I said, 'Whoever you are, be at peace; someone is trying to help,' and nothing more happened and I went to sleep. Incidentally, I do not think this house is haunted. It is probably *me* that is."

Vivian Beresford then went on to talk about the ghostly cats she had seen and the dead husband who has appeared to her, and her Uncle Harry, whom she sent away because she didn't like the look on his face, and several other incidents of communication with the unseen world. I asked her whether all this traffic in her home with the denizens of the netherworld had materially altered her outlook on life.

She thought this over for a moment, then replied: "I have never sought these things, but I cannot really be sorry they have happened, for I know now beyond a shadow of a doubt that death is not death but birth, and a more happy birth than the earthly one, because it is a new and wonderful life—an adventure where I hope we will still be learning, for to curious minds like my own, trying to find out things is even better than knowing. I hope we never know things without the excitement of discovering them."

I have written of Catherine Warren-Browne and her previous life as Catherine Parr, queen to Henry VIII, in an earlier book, *Born Again.* There is no doubt in my mind that her flashes and recurrent dreams of that period are genuine and that she was indeed the one happy wife of Henry VIII, although Mrs. Warren-Browne herself has maintained a healthy skepticism in the matter and has by no means claimed that she was Queen Catherine. In a chapter entitled "Tale of Two Catherines," I have shown why I am so convinced of the authenticity of her experiences. But it is not her reincarnation memories I wish to speak of here, for Catherine Warren-Browne is one of the few people who has had psychic experiences as well as reincarnation flashes. When she heard I was going to visit England and follow up on some of her ghostly adventures, she supplied me with all the necessary data and wrote me a note saying, "Remember me to the rivers, Severn and Wye, and Worcester Cathedral," as lovely a remembrance as anyone can wish. Mrs. Warren-Browne and her husband now live in a modest home near Los Angeles. Once the owners of a large estate, the Warren-Brownes found the battle with taxation too much and decided to quit and go to America. I met Mrs. Warren-Browne several times while I was in Hollywood. The extraordinary experiences which have left her convinced of the reality of a future life started early, when she was only four years old.

"In 1924, when I was four years old," Mrs. Warren-Browne began, "I was sitting by the fire playing when I saw very vividly a picture of a house unknown to me at the time. I saw myself going to the door with my mother, a maid letting us in, and then I saw a huge stone fireplace with a fire burning in it, and a woman in a blue tea gown sitting on a window seat with slightly gray auburn hair. She kissed us, and the maid served tea." At that time Catherine's family lived near Daventry, Northamptonshire.

It was a year later, while her father, a high-ranking naval officer, was overseas with his ship, that her mother took Catherine and her brother to stay with an aunt, Mary McKeever, at Kirkland, Little Malvern, in Worcestershire.

"After Christmas Day," Mrs. Warren-Browne continued her narrative, "my aunt said she was taking us to tea with her old friend Francis Berrington. We went to the house for tea, and everything was as I had seen it in my vision a year before. I had never been to this country before, and Francis Berrington was a friend of my aunt's, not my mother's."

But the most chilling episode in her unusual life happened while she was still a little girl, living at Gloucester House, Malvern Wells, about a mile from her aunt. Not far from there is an artificial hill called the British Camp, also known as the Hereford Beacon. It is situated on the main road from Malvern to Ledbury and is one of the higher hills in the area. The summit of it is terraced and is, in fact, part of the old Roman earthworks which were built in this area.

"I had a very fiery French governess named Chevalier. One afternoon we were walking on the Hereford Beacon and sat down to rest. I remember clearly the sound of sheep cropping the grass and that wonderful scent of juniper. Suddenly I heard the tramping of feet that grew heavier, and over the Malvern Hills to the Beacon came a long line of men marching. We were on the east side of the hill, looking down over the reservoir toward Eastnor Park. There were hundreds of men, some mounted cavalry with a standard-bearer and the rest foot soldiers. I was only six at the time and had not yet started history. The men wore what to me looked like skirts, but there were helmets with plumes and a standard-bearer with a huge bronze-colored eagle. I called to Mademoiselle to hurry and get out of the way and dragged her to one side. She was naturally very shaken, but the men vanished as they reached a certain point of the Beacon. I was fascinated but not afraid, as they seemed quite real. I was sure that we would be walked into, since they marched without breaking line or seeming to give way. But Mademoiselle did not see them. She yanked me home to my aunt's, and I was considered to be ill and was put to bed with aspirin."

Mrs. Warren-Browne's family is Roman Catholic, and the entire area around Malvern is one of the strongholds of English Catholicism. Evidently the family had discussed her strange behavior with a friendly priest, Dom Rodger Huddleston, of a distinguished Roman Catholic family. The following morning, Father Huddleston came to see the little girl.

"As we sat in the garden he talked to me quite casually about what I had seen," Catherine recalls, "and he told me I must have seen 'a picture in time,' for the Roman legions fought a big battle against the Britons and Saxons in this area. He also told me that Cederic, the Saxon leader, was often seen riding when war was about to break out, and that many people in the area had actually seen him."

In 1951, the Warren-Brownes bought a beautiful Cottswold house near the village of Sutton Benger in Wiltshire. Built in 1380, with Tudor additions and three acres of walled gardens, stables, a rose garden, and a pond, it was a most delightful home for them. Their son Giles was away at school in Malvern, daughter Anne was in Bath, and only three-year-old Penelope was with them at the house. After buying the house they brought some fine eighteenth-century furniture into it and hunted for additional pieces to fill odd corners. The house had eight bedrooms, a forty-foot-long lounge hall, a dining room with a perfect early Tudor hearthstone hood, and a very charming drawing room off the hall. Then came a back hall, a butler's pantry, a housekeeper's room in which Mrs. Warren-Browne kept her sewing and linen, and finally a breakfast room with a side door on the lane running alongside the wall where the house joins with the garden wall.

"On November 24, 1951," Mrs. Warren-Browne recalls, "my husband and I returned from Wales. I was five months' pregnant at the time. It was about seven-thirty when we got home, and I was tired. We garaged the car and went indoors. The daily maid, Mrs. Rose Gingell, who lived a mile away, had left supper laid and fires lighted and the heat on. I remember telling my husband, 'What a wonderful house this is; how lucky we are.' He went to get a bottle of wine for our supper, and I went upstairs to bathe Penny and put her to bed. But in spite of the cheerful house, the lights and the fires, there was a terrible cold at the top of the stairs, so I went along the corridor to the older wing to see if a window was open. But they were all closed. I became icy and got a stole to wear, thinking, 'Pregnant women feel odd at times,' but I was very well and happy. I started downstairs. I could hear my husband go from the hall to the dining room. The stairs were shallow oak but carpeted, and as an expectant mother I was particularly careful walking down stairs. So I was going slowly, holding the stair rail, when I felt a very violent push in my back, as if from a hand. I shot halfway down the stairs onto the hall floor, and I know I screamed, as my husband came rushing from the dining room. He helped me to the couch in the hall. I couldn't walk, and the pain was so great he sent for the doctor. It turned out that I had a fractured tibia, fibula, and ankle, and a month later I lost the baby.

"I came home from the hospital in February, after a long siege, but I had to return to the hospital later on for some more surgery. The night before I was due to return to the hospital, I crossed into the hall and saw a bright light on the stairs, sort of bouncing from step to step. The maid was just leaving, so I called out to her and asked whether she knew anything odd about the house. She looked rather uncomfortable and said, 'Well, there have been rumors, and the last two owners only stayed a total of two years each,' but she had seen nothing. A month later I was back home after a rough bout in the hospital. I loved working in the garden, planting new beds, pruning up the old rose garden, and keeping busy about the house. My husband's business sometimes took him away for a day or two. During that time, Penny, the baby, would run screaming from the land-

ing on the stairs, and our son, home from school, reported seeing a woman crying on the landing."

On April 25, 1952, she found herself alone in the
house, the children being away and the little one with
her grandmother. She was getting better and becoming
restless. Before she went home, Rose, the maid, had
prepared supper and brought it up to her room and left
a log fire burning. Mrs. Warren-Browne decided to
read and listen to the radio and then go to sleep.

"I awoke at two in the morning and felt frozen,
although the fire was still burning. I had a heating pad,
but I was still icy and thought I would get some hot milk
and put some brandy in it. Then my dog Towy, a Labra-
dor, who always sleeps by the fire, began to growl and
bristle. I got out of bed and drew the curtains, and the
dog became frantic when I moved from the bed. The
door onto the landing was open, but she would not go
out, so I picked up our large ginger cat from the end of
the bed and thought, If she goes out, I am going out too,
and I tossed the cat into the foyer. It came flying back
at me like a projectile, spitting and screaming. All the
time the cold grew more intense, like an ice barrier. I
shot into bed and stayed put. The next day I thought,
How crazy. I must have been made nervous by the
dog's growling.

"In June, Penny had tonsillitis, so she was put into
the guest room, and I went in there to sleep with her.
It was a lovely room with a vaulted ceiling. The second
night she woke up at two A.M. I give her a drink and
aspirin and she settled down. It was a lovely summer
night, for once. I looked out the window and then went
back to bed and read a little, and finally put the lamp

out. Soon after, the dog began to howl. I sat up and a figure floated through the wall opposite me. I saw the bars of Penny's crib through it. It was luminous but had no real shape. The room was icy and I could feel a sense of awful depression. I thought perhaps it needed prayers, so I said the 'De Profundis.' Instantly, the figure vanished."

A few days later a friend named Duncan Reeves, who knew nothing of these strange happenings, was a guest at the house. Mr. Warren-Browne asked him to get a radio from the room upstairs, but the young man was gone so long that Mrs. Warren-Browne went up after him, wondering what had happened to him.

"When I opened the door, he was holding the bed-post and looking very pale. He said, 'You have an odd bedroom,' and explained he had seen a thing similar to what I had seen in the guest room, only it went upward and through the ceiling. After this I felt I was not crazy and told our doctor about it. Dr. Hicks suggested we call our parish priest. Father Hickey came and very matter-of-factly went through the exorcism ritual in the hope that it would end the matter once and for all. On asking around, it turned out that we had about the most haunted house in Wiltshire."

Apparently, the ghost was of the obstinate kind. A little later a Dominican priest from New Zealand, a friend of the family, noticed that there was something odd about the house and suggested blessing the house again. Not much later, the Warren-Brownes sold the house to a family from Yorkshire with eight children. Mrs. Warren-Browne was sure that the children would frighten the ghost away, but they only stayed one year.

Eventually the house was turned into a hotel, and if the guests have seen the ghosts and vice versa, they haven't said anything about it.

Mrs. Lilly Raymond is in her early sixties and a retired secretary. She is, in her own words, "quite sane and not an imaginative person," but the experience she went through in 1966 has quite unsettled her. Two of her grandchildren, a boy of six and a girl of three, were staying with her at the time in her house in Essex and were sleeping in her front room. One particular night the boy seemed restless and came into Mrs. Raymond's bedroom at two o'clock in the morning and again at two-thirty. When she tried to take him back to bed, he was reluctant to leave her. He then complained that he had been hearing "funny music," and as he was telling her about it, he held her hand very tightly and said, "Listen!"

"I then heard for myself the strange tinkly sound of a piano on which five notes only were repeatedly played. Not wishing to alarm the child in any way, I told him that it was somebody in the road having a party, but he immediately said, 'This isn't party music, as it keeps playing the same thing over and over again.' I stayed in the room the rest of the night, and several times more I heard the same five notes so sadly repeated."

The following morning she talked to a neighbor and inquired about previous tenants of the house and in particular if anybody had ever played the piano. It was thus that she learned about a certain Mrs. McKay who had lived in the house fifty years before her. Mrs.

McKay's husband was in the merchant navy and often away. One of her twin sons died rather suddenly at age ten, followed a few months later by the demise of the other in a bicycle accident. Mrs. McKay became a diabetic and passed away in the very same year. Mrs. Raymond also discovered that the woman living in the apartment above hers hears the music continuously at different times of the day. Apparently, the succession of tragedies in Mrs. McKay's life unhinged her mind to the point where she was unable to leave: it was her piano, long gone from the flat, that the ladies kept hearing.

A few years ago a ghost made local newspaper headlines by keeping a man from going to jail. The story concerned a certain William Haywood, in his twenties, of Dunstable, Bedfordshire, who was in court for repeated traffic offenses. He was about to be sentenced when his attorney stepped forward and explained that there were special reasons why this man should not be sent to prison. Apparently Mr. Haywood lived in a haunted house, and Mrs. Haywood was so terrified of the specter that she could not possibly be left alone in the two-hundred-year-old house.

Mrs. Valerie Haywood explained that she had seen the ghost many times. "He is an old man dressed in rustic black Victorian clothes, with a gold stud at his collar. He appears in the bedroom at seven or eight o'clock at night. He just stands there in the room; he doesn't look evil, but he terrifies me. Even our dog won't go into the room; she whimpers when she passes the room."

Since the Haywoods had a small baby, they did not

feel like moving out of the house. An exorcism was held, but apparently it did no good. William Haywood has also seen the ghost and called him the "man in black." As a last resort, they simply moved out of the bedroom and closed it off from the rest of the house. They asked around the neighborhood and learned that the description of the ghost fit a man who used to live in the house who had gone insane in that very bedroom.

The magistrate appreciated the Haywoods' predicament and fined the husband instead of sending him to jail.

In Yorkshire a woman by the name of Betty Hanwood will never again touch a ouija board.

She and a friend were operating the ouija board, not really believing in it, but enjoying it as a game.

One Saturday in July in the late 1960's, the board began spelling a lot of nonsense, but then came an order to get hold of a pen so "it" could draw a map. Since both Mrs. Hanwood and her friend had used automatic writing before, they assumed that the entity, whoever he was, preferred the quicker method of automatic writing in his intended communication. So they took a pad and put their fingers onto the pen, waiting for a message. The unseen force drew a map of a road, putting a church on one side and what appeared to be old stocks and mounting steps. It drew a tree in a churchyard and a compass and little tracks from the south part of the compass and wrote "forty paces." Then it drew some coins and a dagger and ordered them to go find them. Mrs. Hanwood demanded to know who the communicator was, and the pen wrote the name, "Albert Gemside." The communicator then confided that he had died in 1673 and that his gravestone was in the churchyard. Mrs. Hanwood recognized the church from the drawing as the church at nearby Mastshead, not far from her own village of Roberttown. Still, it was too far to walk, especially as her young friend, Steven, could not walk great distances.

"Anyway, we put it all down as usual to the outpourings of our subconscious minds," Mrs. Hanwood explained, "as this was the way we treated things that came from the board. We promptly forgot about it, but we kept all the records. The following day my friend came over again and we took out the board. Immediately it spelled out, 'You didn't believe me; you didn't go!' I talked back to the board, explaining that it was too far; then the board demanded pen and paper again and informed us, 'I will draw you another map nearer at hand.' When we put the pen to paper, it started drawing a road and even put the white lines in the center. It drew a square object at one side of the road and a cow at the other. In front of the cow it made a cross and banged on the cross several times."

Mrs. Hanwood asked what the square object was, and the communicator replied "iron thing." Mrs. Hanwood objected that she didn't understand, so the pen drew an electric pylon. Immediately Mrs. Hanwood objected again, for if this was the personality of a man who had died in 1673, he would not know what a pylon was.

"I asked where it was, and the pen drew an arrow pointing one way and wrote 'Roberttown,' and another pointing the other and wrote 'Robin.' When we had established where it was, I asked what was there, and it drew five coins—one with a hole in the middle—and a key. I asked what kind of coins they were, and it wrote four English and one *pfennig* and then it wrote in very large letters, 'Go now!' "

Even though her husband looked at her as though she were mad, Mrs. Hanwood decided to take the unseen up on his offer. In the company of her mother-in-law, they set out just as the map had indicated, feeling sure that it would all be a wild ghost chase. When they got to the road the pen had drawn, sure enough, there, opposite the pylon in the field, was one black cow, standing exactly where the pen had indicated.

"I nearly died with shock. We went across toward the cow, and just to one side was a telegraph pole. I started to pull the grass away from the wall, but something inside my head said, No, Betty, not there, move over to the cow. I did this and the cow turned and faced us and never once took its eyes from us. I bent down and pulled the grass away and there just under the soil was a key."

With trembling hands Mrs. Hanwood started to dig, scraping away at the hole. There was a little pile of coins, just as the communicator had indicated. When they returned and threw the coins on the table, her husband turned pale. Immediately they picked up the pen. It wrote, "Now do you believe me?"

The incident kept bothering Mrs. Hanwood. She asked people about its significance, even wrote to the manufacturer of the ouija board, but no one could give her a satisfactory answer. Finally, she went to see a clairvoyant, who touched the coins and immediately informed her that they had once belonged to a shepherd but that they had been put into the ground for her to find. She instructed Mrs. Hanwood to take them back and put them back into the ground again. Without questioning the clairvoyant, Mrs. Hanwood buried the key and the coins in her garden. She told no one about it, but she marked the exact spot. A few days later she told the entire story to a friend who is also interested in psychical research. The friend wanted to see the coins and the key. After a while, Mrs. Hanwood agreed to dig up the coins. She took the spade and went back to the spot she alone knew, but key and coins had disappeared. There was no logical explanation for this: they could not have sunk into the ground in so short a time, and no one else knew that she had placed them there.

"I am more unsettled now than I was when I first found them," she explained. "I have plenty of witnesses to all of it, but the clairvoyant told me to destroy the ouija board and burn all the maps, and I took her advice, so there is really nothing I have to show for it."

I imagine Albert Gemside, the prankster from the seventeenth century, must have had quite a laugh at the expense of those incredulous twentieth-century types who dig for treasure and then let it slip out of their hands!

Mrs. Margaret W. is the wife of an executive of a major company and the mother of a thirty-two-year-old son. Until the age of twenty-six she worked as a medical librarian and secretary, and even now she is active in community work and women's clubs: the very image of a proper midwestern lady. In September, 1968, Mr. and

Mrs. W. decided to visit a childhood friend who is a medical doctor and lives with her husband in a large country manor near Keighley, Yorkshire. The house was built in 1742 and has three stories. One moning, toward five o'clock, Mrs. W. awoke and decided to go to the bathroom, which was situated to the left of the second-floor bedroom. The bedroom faced the stairs. Mrs. W. opened the bedroom door and stepped out into the hall. She didn't bother to put on her robe. Imagine her surprise when she looked up and saw a man standing there, looking at her. He was just as surprised as Mrs. W. was. The man was about to go up the next flight of stairs, and apparently Mrs. W.'s appearance had startled him. She noticed that he was about sixty years of age, with gray hair cut to shoulder length, and that he wore a hat not unlike a Quaker's. He was dressed all in black with the exception of a small white tie or collar, and he also wore a cape. Quickly Mrs. W. stepped back into the bedroom, slamming the door behind her, and got back into bed. She discussed the experience with her husband, who assured her that she must have been asleep and dreamed the whole thing. They decided not to tell their hosts, on the off chance that Mrs. W. had indeed seen a man, and that he was simply someone who visited the home regularly.

A year later, Nancy S. and her husband returned the visit paid them the previous year by the W's. As they were sitting around the table talking about their various experiences, Mrs. W. finally mentioned "the man in black" and wondered who he was, still assuming that he had been someone friendly with her hosts in Yorkshire. The English couple were stunned: they explained that the man in black was a ghost. It seems that they had first encountered the gentleman while entertaining some guests one evening. The man in black, looking exactly the way Mrs. W. had described him, suddenly appeared out of nowhere, opening a door where there was none, walked across the parlor, opened the door and walked out into the kitchen. They were still trying to find out who he was and why he kept coming back to the house.

Raynham Hall, Fakenham, Norfork, is the ancestral seat of the Townshend family and is open to the public but one day a year. Evidently the Townshends do not particularly like ordinary visitors tramping through the grounds. They do not even like psychic visitors like myself coming up and having a look at the famous Brown Lady who keeps reappearing in various parts of the house. In the official guidebook written by the marquess himself, it is said that Lady Dorothy Walpole, sister of the famous British politician and prime minister, died of smallpox in 1726. But it is also true that the family had difficulties with her, that her children were taken away from her at one time, and that for part of her life she lived at nearby Houghton Hall. Traditionally, she's said to have died of "an unsound mind," shut up in one of the upper stories at Raynham Hall, and is therefore haunting the Hall. This particular ghost came into worldwide prominence in 1936 when two professional photographers were taking pictures at Raynham Hall, not in order to photograph the ghost, but on a commission from the owners who wanted their celebrated and art-filled country seat recorded for posterity. Picture the photographer's surprise when one of them insisted he saw a "white lady" walking down the main staircase. The other photographer, not being psychic, did not see anything, but he encouraged his colleague to snap a picture of what he saw. The result was the famous "Brown Lady of Raynham Hall,"* which first appeared in *Country Gentlemen*, later in *Life*, and in dozens of other publications, including one of my own. It is probably the first fully authenticated photograph of a ghost.

About that time Lady Townshend held a seance to help quiet the restless spirit of Lady Walpole, but either Lady Walpole didn't wish to be quieted or the seance lacked the proper ingredients. The ghost keeps reappearing from time to time, and she has been observed on the staircase, by the nursery, and looking through the windows.

Back in 1966, Mrs. Ellen Parsons lived in the immediate area of Raynham Hall. Her husband was in the air force, and she had ample opportunity to strike up acquaintanceships with the people in the village. This enabled her to get a private tour of the Hall. She didn't encounter the Brown Lady in the Hall itself, but one evening, at the—to her—appropriate hour of midnight, she went together with a friend to the side where a rose garden skirts the Hall. After peering out toward the Hall for a while, the two ladies saw a black shape, about the height of a woman, swaying back and forth. They ran toward it, but when they reached the spot where

*The ghost is known as the "Brown Lady" because of the color of the dress she wears in a painting upstairs at the Hall.

they had seen the apparition, all they could find was a knee-high rose bush. I guess Lady Walpole, or rather I should say, Lady Townshend, for that was her married name, just wasn't receiving that evening.

One of the strangest ghost hunts I have ever undertaken started innocently enough when I received a letter from a young woman by the name of Marion Turner who lived with her mother in the coastal area west of Manchester. Both Miss Turner and her mother are psychic and have had encounters with ghosts and apparitions in several houses through the years.

Lowther Grange is a former mansion turned into small flats which the owner, a certain Mrs. Gardener, was in the habit of renting out. One day Miss Turner and her mother placed an advertisement in the local evening paper seeking a place to live near St. Anne's. The ad was responded to by Mrs. Gardener, and the two ladies were offered a permanent home because, as Mrs. Gardener put it, she was passionately fond of the name of Turner. It so happened that several previous owners of the house were also named Turner, and Mrs. Gardener herself was related to some of them. Thus it came to pass that the two ladies moved into the house at St. Anne's, looking forward to many years of residence. One morning, Mrs. Gardener offered the two ladies a tour of the house, seeing that there were a number of vacant rooms, and the two ladies eagerly accepted. When they entered one of these vacant rooms, it appeared rather dark to Marion Turner, and she had the strangest feeling that she was walking into a scene from an earlier age.

"Two elderly men of the Victorian or Edwardian era," she explained, "were involved in a bitter quarrel concerning the property. The men could have been brothers, and one very probably had lost the goods to the other, so a bitter and violent argument ensued. One of the two men raised a clenched fist toward the other, shouting abuse, threatening to throw the other man out if he refused to leave at once, and ended with, 'And take your blasted trunk with you!' As I left this room, the awful feeling gradually subsided, but it troubles me still."

Naturally Marion Turner's curiosity was aroused. She went to the local library but found herself frustrated at every turn in trying to pin down the actual event that she had clairvoyantly relived. Finally, with the help of one Kathleen Eyres, an author of historical books dealing with the area, she discovered that a certain Harry Clifford Turner had lived in the house, which he owned, in the year 1910. He had the reputation of being a tight landlord, and of having dealt rather roughly with tenants unable to fulfill their obligations.

Miss Turner had another ghostly experience in a house they later moved to at 19 Bamton Avenue, Blackpool. From the description Miss Turner was able to give the historian, she was able to pinpoint the man's identity. All this sounded so enticing, I decided to pay the area a visit. I had arranged with the two ladies to meet me at the Manchester Airport. Sure enough, there they were sitting on a bench, looking a little uncertain, for it turned out that they had never been inside an airport before, nor for that matter had they ever left their native county, not even to go to London. I had also asked the renowned British medium James Gardner (no relation to Mrs. Gardener), who lived not far from Manchester, to meet us at the airport. Unfortunately he was unable to do so. I hired a cab, and we set out to visit the house where Miss Turner had seen the two ghosts quarrel. It was a good hour to an hour and a half, riding in a city cab, with the two ladies staring at me and occasionally answering questions about their former home. We had picked up the medium, Mr. Gardner, and now we were ready to enter the mysterious-looking mansion to make contact with the ghosts, if possible. It was then that I discovered that the ladies Turner had neglected to notify the owner of our impending arrival! "Don't worry," Mrs. Turner said, assuring me that she could straighten things out in a hurry. Unfortunately, the owner's wife had died a short time before, and the owner was in no mood to talk to ghost-hunters. Try as I might, offering him anything from condolences to money, I could not budge him to allow us inside the house. Since an Englishman's house is his castle, there was nothing to do but leave. Another forty-five minutes or so later, we arrived at the house on Bamton Avenue. The present owner was a little friendlier here and invited us inside, even though we were strangers to her. The house on Bamton Avenue was one of those simple frame houses people of moderate income live in, two stories high, surrounded by a little garden, and generally in need of repairs. On Miss Turner's prompting we walked up the stairs into the kitchen on the second floor: apparently the house had once been divided into two apartments, so there was an upstairs kitchen. It was here that Miss Turner had had the experience. Only, it now turned out, the experience wasn't in *this* house— it was in the house across the street. And what was that experience? Apparently the two ladies had observed a sickly-looking woman in the little house directly across from them who kept staring at them from behind the curtains. She was wearing a nightgown and looking odd. Marion Turner saw her many times and remarked to her mother how sunken the woman's eyes seemed to be and that she was probably not well. Eventually, the ladies' curiosity got the better of them and they decided to find out from a shopkeeper who the sad-looking stranger across the street really was. "What lady?" the shopkeeper wanted to know. "That house has been empty for years." It couldn't be, the two ladies replied. Then they described the woman they had seen in the house. The shopkeeper's eyebrows rose several inches. "That woman," he said slowly, "that woman died several years ago."

I decided that this hadn't been my most fortuitous journey, and the sooner I got back to London the better. On our way back to Manchester, we dropped off Jim Gardner, who invited us in for tea. When I offered him his usual fee, he politely refused. Jim Gardner had the reputation of being one of the finer trance mediums of the past twenty years. In fact, Alexander Sanders had first told me of him, and pointed out that Mr. Gardner was also a materialization medium. When I brought up the question of sitting for materializations, Mr. Gardner explained that his health no longer permitted him to do so, but that he had indeed produced ectoplasm in his earlier seances. I thanked him and his wife for their hospitality and the excellent tea and expressed my hope that on some future occasion we would indeed come face to face with a ghost—or at the very least, a landlord who wouldn't mind our looking for one.

6
THE GHOST ON TELEVISION

Until 1965 I had heard of two kinds of ghosts connected with television: those impersonated by actors and those caused by the interference of tall buildings. Now I was to learn of still another kind of ghost on television, this one being the real McCoy. It all started with a lecture I gave at the British College of Psychic Studies in London in 1965. After my lecture on ghosts, which was illustrated by slides of apparitions, I was approached by a tall, intellectual-looking lady who wanted to tell me about a very strange haunted house in East Anglia. This was my first meeting with Ruth Plant, who explained that she was a writer and researcher, with a background in social science. Her beliefs lay in the Spiritualist philosophy, and she had had any number of psychic experiences herself. I asked her to drop me a note about the house in East Anglia. I expected it to be just another haunted house, probably containing the usual complement of footsteps, doors opening or closing by themselves, or possibly even an apparition of a deceased relative. By *my* standards, that constitutes a classic, conventional haunting.

The following January, Miss Plant lived up to her promise. She explained that the house in East Anglia was called Morley Old Hall, and though it was principally of the Stuart period, it stood on much earlier foundations, going back to pre-Saxon times. It was situated near Norwich in the northeast of England and apparently belonged to a friend of hers who had bought it with a view to restoring it. It had been in lamentable condition and not suitable to be lived in. Her friend, by the name of Ricky Cotterill, was essentially a pig farmer; nevertheless, he and his young wife and their baby managed to live in the sprawling mansion, or rather in that part of it which he had been able to restore on his own funds, and the excitement of living with so much history more than adequately made up for the deprivations he was subjecting himself to. Miss Plant explained that the house was way off the beaten track and was, in fact, hard to find unless one knew the countryside. There were two moats around it, and archeological digs had been undertaken all over that part of the country for many years, since that part of East Anglia is one of the oldest and most historic sections of England.

At the time of her first communication with me, in January, 1966, Miss Plant had not as yet undertaken any research into the background of the house or its surroundings. She thought the house worthy of my attention because of what had happened to her and a friend during a visit.

"I went to stay there with a Norwegian friend, Anne Wilhelmsen, whose father was a cultural attaché of Norway in London, and who was herself a university graduate," Ruth Plant explained. "This was two years ago at Easter. We had intended to stay at the local hotel, but Mr. Cotterill, the owner of the mansion, found that the hotel was entirely full."

Under the circumstances, the owner moved out of the room he had been occupying and let the two ladies use it for the night. As he knew of Miss Plant's interest in ghosts, he assured her that to the best of his knowledge there were no ghosts there, since he had lived there for three years and had seen nothing. As a matter of fact, the two ladies slept well, and in the morning Miss Plant got up and walked across the big room connecting the two wings with the kitchen, all of it being on the first floor.

"When I came back, I felt impressed to pause at the large window which looked down the front drive, in spite of the fact that it had no glass in it and the day was bitterly cold. I felt very peaceful and contemplative and I suddenly heard a Catholic prayer, the Hail Mary, and was sure that the 'presence' I felt was that of the lady of the house. After I had noted this, I went back into our bedroom and was surprised to find Anne sitting up in bed looking very worried. She said she had just heard the rustle of bedclothes and heavy breathing while she lay there. She had sat up in bed to listen more closely, and immediately the sound ceased, only to come back again when she lay down. We told our host about this over breakfast, but he could not enlighten us further. So I went into the village and in talking to people found out that several people who had lived in the house had experienced very much the same thing. One man had actually seen the lady quite clearly at the window, and others had heard her, like Anne."

The "Lady at the Window" fascinated Ruth Plant, especially as she didn't know her identity. As was her custom then, and is now, she decided to have a sitting with a reputable medium to see whether the medium might pick up something spiritual around her and possibly shed some light on the identity of the lady ghost of Morley Old Hall. This time she had a sitting with a certain Mr. Bogoran, one of the regulars sitting at the College of Psychic Studies, Queensbury Place. "I didn't mention anything about the ghost, but said I had a friend who was trying to restore a beautiful old Stuart house and I wondered if anyone on the Other Side could offer any helpful advice."

Instead of advice on how to restore the house, medium Bogoran described the house itself in minute detail and then added that he saw a ghostly lady standing at one of the windows. This of course came as a surprise to Miss Plant, but even more of a shock was in store for her: Mr. Bogoran volunteered two additional statements of interest. One, that the owner of the house, her friend, would be on television within a few weeks, and two, that there was another ghost in the house, a monk who was attached to the house, not because he had been happy there like the ghostly lady, but because he had been involved in a killing.

Since Mr. Cotterill, the owner of the house, had

absolutely no connection with television, the first statement evoked nothing but doubt in Ruth Plant's mind. Picture her surprise when several days after her sitting with Mr. Bogoran, Ricky Cotterill telephoned to tell her that he had been approached by a local television station to have an all-night session at the house which would be filmed for television. The reason for his call was to invite her to Norwich to appear as part of the program. In the excitement of this development, Ruth Plant forgot all about the ghostly monk.

When she arrived at the Hall, she met Tony Cornell, a psychic researcher from Cambridge. Ruth and Mr. Cornell did not see things the same way: she sensed him to be skeptical and negative and suspected his presence in the house was more to debunk the ghosts than to find them. It turned out later that Mr. Cornell was, as the program producer put it, "Our handiest accredited psychic investigator," called into the case not necessarily because of his commitment to the reality of ghosts, but because his offices were not too far away, and time was of the essence. Ruth brought along a sound tape of her sitting with Mr. Bogoran, but it was not used in the film. She gave the required interview and thought no more about it. A few weeks later, the filmed report of Morley Old Hall went on the air. Ruth Plant saw it at a local hotel, where it was rather badly focused, and she could hardly recognize herself or anyone else. Nevertheless, something odd happened during that screening.

"During the performance, there was a loud bang on the set," Ruth Plant stated, "which seemed to have no normal cause. My basset hound, who had been fast asleep with her back to the screen, jumped up in great apprehension and stood gazing at the screen as though she saw *someone we could not see.*"

A few days later Ruth Plant telephoned Mr. Cotterill, and it was only then that she heard the amazing results of the television of the film. It appeared that no fewer than twenty-three people from the general public had written into the broadcasting station and asked who the bearded monk was, standing behind Mr. Cornell while he was speaking!

Now no one had mentioned anything about a ghostly monk, but everyone connected with the venture knew that a ghostly *lady* had been observed by a number of witnesses. Consequently, she would have been on the minds of those participating in the experiment, if a mind picture could indeed find its way onto a television film.

The idea of a ghost appearing on television naturally excited me. Immediately I got in touch with Michael Robson, producer of the documentary and one of the executives of Anglia Television. Michael Robson, who had been to Morley Old Hall many times before the documentary was made, offered to let me see the actual film when I came to England. "Our film unit had an all-night vigil in the Hall," he explained in a statement dated September 2, 1966, "with the chairman of the Cambridge Psychical Research and Spontaneous Cases Committee, Mr. Tony Cornell. Various things of interest occurred during the night, in particular a moving tumbler, but what caused all the excitement was this: Mr. Cornell and I were discussing the Hall on film by a mullioned window as dawn was breaking. No sooner had the film been transmitted than a great many people wrote in asking who the figure was that appeared between Mr. Cornell and myself. All their descriptions were the same: the face and trunk of a monkish-type figure looking between us. Mr. Cornell and I examined the film closely afterwards ourselves and saw nothing: but in view of the large number of people who claimed to have seen the figure, Mr. Cornell thought it an interesting example of collective hallucination, and took away the letters for closer study."

It turned out that Mr. Cornell was not a parapsychologist with an academic connection, but merely an interested ghost-fancier. With the help of Miss Plant, and considerable patience, I managed to obtain the letters which Mr. Cornell had taken with him and examined them myself. His explanation of the phenomenon as a "mass hallucination" is, of course, an easy way out of coming to grips with the problem itself—a genuine psychic phenomenon. But the twenty-three witnesses are far more eloquent in their description of what they experienced than any would-be scientist could possibly be in trying to explain away the phenomenon.

Mrs. Joan Buchan of Great Yarmouth wrote: "My husband and I saw a figure of a monk with a cowl over his head and with his hands clasped as though in prayer. It could be seen quite clearly, standing quietly in the window. It didn't appear to be looking at the men conversing, but behind them."

"I saw the figure of a man which appeared to me to be that of a monk; he had on a round hat, a long cloak, and his hands were together as in prayer," observed Miss A. Hewitt of Southrepps.

"I saw the figure quite distinctly, considering I only

have a twelve-inch screen and the sunlight was pouring into my room. The figure appeared behind the profile of the man who was talking, as if looking through the window," stated L. M. Gowing. "I thought perhaps it was due to the light, but the man talking moved and seemed to partly cover it. When he went back to his former position, it was there clearer than before."

"Both my daughter and myself certainly saw the outline of a priest to the right of the speaker and to the left of the interviewer," wrote Mrs. G. D. Hayden of Bromham. Not only did Mr. and Mrs. Carter of Lincolnshire say, "It was very clear," but Mrs. Carter sent in a drawing of the monk she had seen on the television. From Norwich, where the broadcast originated, came a statement from a viewer named Elviera Panetta who also drew the bearded monk, showing him to have a long, haggard face. "Both my mother and I saw the monk looking through the window; he is cowled, bearded, and his hands are slightly raised." One viewer, Miss M. C. Grix, wrote to the station inquiring whether "it was a real person standing in the window just behind the man who was talking, dressed in black and looking as if he had his hands together in prayer," to which Nora Kononenko of Suffolk added, "It first looked to me like a skull with a hood, and then, as the gentlemen went on talking, it seemed to come forward and peer in. At that moment it distinctly changed into a gaunt-looking face, with a horrible leer upon it." The station decided to run the film again, as testimonies kept pouring in. After the second run, even more people saw the ghostly monk on the screen.

"Your repeat of the alleged haunted house shook

me considerably," wrote Mrs. A. C. Mason, "not because of what I had seen in the original broadcast, but because your Mr. MacGregor gaily quipped, 'Well, did you see anything?' I was astonished that anyone else *couldn't* see what was so clear to me. I did see the monk both times." Some viewers sent in simple statements, unsolicited and to the point. "I saw the monk in the window just as plain as could be. It was there at the time and I can assure you I did not imagine it," wrote Mrs. Joan Collis of Suffolk.

"He didn't seem to be hooded but had long hair and was bearded," stated Mrs. Janet Halls of Norwich, and Mrs. F. Nicolaisen of Cambridge volunteered that "I had seen the figure on the previous showing but didn't mention it for fear of being laughed at. This time I traced it out for my husband, but he still couldn't see it, much to my annoyance."

If all these people were suffering from mass hallucination, it is certainly strange that they hallucinated in so many different ways, for many of the reports differed in slight but important details. "Towards the end of the showing, my sister and I distinctly saw an image of a cowled monk from head to waist," wrote Miss W. Caplen of Lowestoft. Probably Mrs. J. G. Watt of Cambridge put it best when she wrote, "I had no idea what sort of ghost I was expected to look for, and I saw nothing until the two men were discussing the house. But outside the window I then saw clearly, behind them, the figure of a monk. He wore a monk's habit and was bare-headed, with the monk's haircut associated with the monks of olden days, bald patch with fringe, either fair or gray hair. His face was that of a young man and he had a very serene look on his face. His arms were hanging down in front of him, with his right hand placed lightly on top of his left. I saw this all very plainly and naturally and I thought everyone else would be able to, so I thought the television people were having a game with the viewers, and I thought it was all a hoax. Next day a friend told me of Anglia TV's purpose of rerunning the film, and I realized it was serious. The strange thing is that our television set is not what it used to be, and we don't get a good picture—and yet I saw this monk very clearly."

By now it was clear to me that twenty-three people —or at last count thirty-one—had actually seen or thought they had seen the figure of a monk where none was supposed to be. Many others, if not the majority of viewers, however, did not see the monk. Obviously, then, it was on the film, and yet visible only to those with psychic gifts. This raised interesting questions: while we know that ghosts appear only to those capable of seeing them, can apparitions also be photographed selectively, so that they can be seen only by those who are psychic, while others not so gifted will not be able to see them in the photograph or film? Also, was the case of the ghost on television unique, or are there other such instances on the record?

According to the *London Express* of December 19, 1969, five shop girls saw a ghostly figure on a closed-circuit TV set. "The girls and customers watched fascinated for forty-five minutes as the figure of a woman in a long Victorian dress stood at the top of the stairs in the boutique in High Street, Kent, occasionally waving her hand and patting her hair. Several times the figure walked halfway down the stairs and then went back up again to the upper floor of the boutique, which had been converted only a few months ago from an old house." The first one to see the ghostly apparition on the closed-circuit television setup was eighteen-year-old Sally White, who pointed her out to her colleague, Janet Abbs, saying, "You've got a customer." But Janet Abbs walked right through the figure. One of the other girls, Andree Weller, said "As the figure went upstairs it disappeared into a sort of mist and then reappeared again." The incident happened at lunchtime, and though five girls saw the woman, when they walked upstairs where they had seen her, they found the place empty. When they returned downstairs and looked at the screen, there was the ghost again. Unlike the monk of Morley Old Hall, who appeared for only a few seconds on screen, the Victorian lady of High Street, Chatham, Kent, stayed for a whole hour, apparently enjoying her performance hugely.

However, what none of the viewers who had written in had pointed out was the fact that the figure of the monk was not in proportion to the size of the two flesh-and-blood people talking on the screen at the time: the monk seemed considerably smaller than they were. Ruth Plant found the emergence of the second ghost most exciting. She decided to consult two other London mediums, to see whether they might pick up something concerning his identity. One of them was Trixie Allingham, who immediately "saw" a ghostly monk around the house and informed Ruth that he had been attacked by someone who came in while he was praying. The monk had defended himself by striking the intruder with a chalice. She felt that the priest, with the help of a soldier, had later buried the body and the chalice. George Southhal, primarily a dowsing medium, volunteered that there was a chalice buried on the premises and described a set of cups, the largest of which was reserved for a man of importance. He saw Morley as a place similar to a pilgrims' retreat. At the time of Miss Plant's sitting with George Southhal, neither of them knew as yet that it had been a little-known pre-Reformation practice to give a special chalice to a prior or bishop, since he was not supposed to use the chalice used by ordinary priests. All the mediums Ruth Plant sat with were emphatic about some buried treasure and secret passages leading from the house to a nearby church. The latter could be confirmed during later research. As for the treasure, it hasn't been found yet, but the effort continues.

I decided to arrange for a visit to Norfolk at the earliest opportunity. That opportunity presented itself in September of 1966 when a film producer offered to come with me to inspect potential sites for a documentary motion-picture. I suggested Morley Old Hall and notified Ruth Plant to get everything ready: arrange for a visit to the Hall, suggest a suitable hotel nearby, notify Anglia TV of our desire to see the controversial television documentary, and, finally, to make everybody happy, let the local press have a go at us—the American ghost-hunter and his entourage paying a call to the local ghost. Miss Plant was to serve as technical advisor to the film. (Unfortunately, the film was never made, because the producer and I could not see eye to eye on a treatment that would allow the story to be told in exciting but scientifically valid terms.)

We rode up to Norwich from London. The projected film producer, Gilbert Cates, who was a firm nonbeliever, could not see how such things as ghosts were possible, while the third member of the party, the distinguished motion picture scenarist Victor Wolfson, argued equally strongly that such things as spirits were indeed not only possible but likely. At one point the discussion got so heated that I began to worry whether we would ever arrive together in Norfolk. Finally, Victor Wolfson changed the subject. With a shrug, he commented, "I don't think I can convince Gil. He's underdeveloped." Gil, a good sport under all circumstances, smiled. As for me, I began to wonder about the wisdom of having brought my two fellow adventurers at all.

Ruth Plant had advised us to bed down for the night in Norfolk, but my producer friend was so eager to be close to the "action" that he insisted we stay at the little Abbey Hotel at Wyndmondham, which is very near to Morley. We arrived at the hotel, tired and dirty, just in time to have an evening meal.

Waking early, I looked out onto the church and cemetery below my windows. It seemed very peaceful and far removed from any ghostly encounters. I took a look at a local map supplied to me by Ruth Plant. The city of Norwich, where we would view the television film, was nine miles to the east, while Morley Old Hall was a little over twelve miles to the west.

The abbey church at Wyndmondham was an impressive edifice for a village of this small size. Early in the twelfth century, William D'Albini, who had been given the town and manor of Wyndmondham, which included Morley, for his help with the Norman invasion of England, established here a monastery consisting of a prior and twelve Benedictine monks. The Benedictines, wearing black habits, were the most aristocratic and wealthy of all the religious orders, and, because of that, frequently came into conflict with poorer, humbler religious orders. It also appeared that Richard, William's brother, was made Abbot of St. Alban's, in Hertfordshire, one of the largest Benedictine monasteries in England, and Wyndmondham was a sort of daughter house to St. Alban's.

"But the relationship between the two houses was never good, and the jealousies and rivalries between them only ceased when, in 1448, Wyndmondham became an abbey in its own right," writes the Reverend J. G. Tansley Thomas in his *History of Wyndmondham Abbey.* I had the occasion to study all this while waiting for the car to pick me up for the short journey to Morley Old Hall.

After twenty minutes or so, there appeared a clump of bushes, followed by tall trees—trees that showed their age and the fact that they had not been interfered with for many years. All sorts of trees were growing wild here, and as the road rounded a bend, they seemed to swallow us up. We rumbled over a wooden bridge crossing a deep and pungent moat. Directly behind it was a brick breastwork, overgrown by all sorts of plants. This was the second, inner moat, I was told later; the outer moat was farther back and scarcely noticeable today, although in Saxon times it was a major bulwark. The car stopped in front of the imposing mansion, built of red brick and topped off by grayish-blue shingles in the manner of the seventeenth century. Part of the surrounding wall was still standing, and there were two very tall trees inside the inner moat, which gave Morley Old Hall a particularly romantic appearance. The Hall rises three stories, and windows had been replaced in many of them, attesting to the owner's skill at restoring what he had bought as a virtual ruin. We walked up a beautifully restored staircase, to the second story, where the Cotterill family lived at the time. Much of the mansion was still uninhabitable. Some rooms consisted of bare walls, while others still had ancient fireplaces in them, staring at the visitor like toothless monsters.

Ruth Plant had managed to arrange it so that the principal witnesses to the phenomena at the Hall would be present for my interrogation, and so it was that we assembled upstairs in the library—not the magnificent Stuart library of old, but a reasonable facsimile. I first turned to Frank Warren, a man in his middle seventies who had once lived in the house, long before it passed into the present owner's hands. He had come from the nearby village to talk to me, and later I paid a courtesy call on his little cottage, adorned with beautiful flowers from one end to the other: Frank Warren was, and is, a dedicated gardener. Like so many people of the area, he is "fay," that is, psychic, and he recalls vividly how he saw and actually touched his pet dog two months after the animal had died. But the human ghost at Morley Old Hall was another matter.

"I was working in the garden," he began, "and the lady of the house said, 'I wish you'd clip around that window; those pieces annoy me.' So I started to clip. It was a beautiful day, with the sun shining. All at once, just like that, there appeared a lady in the window, as close to me as you are and she looked at me. She was tall, and I noticed every detail of her dress. She looked at me and the expression on her face never changed. Her lips never moved and I thought to myself, 'I can't stand it. I'll go and do some work in the vegetable garden.' When I returned she was gone, so I completed my job at the window. Well, I used to go and have a meal with the housekeeper. I said, 'There is something I'd like you to tell me: who is the other lady living in this house?'

" 'Well,' she replied, 'there is no other lady living in this house. You know exactly who is in this house.' I replied that I didn't, because I had seen somebody here I had never seen before."

Apparently the housekeeper was frightened by the idea of having ghosts about the place, for Lady Ironside, who was then the owner of the Hall, summoned the gardener about the matter. "I can't help it," he replied to her protestations. "I saw her with my own eyes." It was wartime and Lady Ironside was hard put to keep servants about the place, so she asked the gardener please to keep quiet about the ghost.

"Did you ever see the lady ghost again?" I inquired.

"A fortnight afterwards I went past the other window, on the opposite side, and there sat the housekeeper reading a book, and beside her sat the same lady. The housekeeper didn't see her. She wore a plain black dress, which seemed a bit stiff and went right to the ground, so I couldn't see her feet. I had a quarter of an hour to examine her, and I didn't see her feet."

Gordon Armstrong had come from London to talk to us at Morley Old Hall. "This is my second visit," he began. "I was here toward the end of July last year, 1965. I was working in London at the time and hitch-hiked my way through the night and arrived at Morley in the small hours of the morning. Having walked up the road, I came into the house—it must have been somewhere around two o'clock in the morning—and at the time I had already heard of a ghost being there, or rumored to be there, so I was half expecting to see one. Of course, I had never seen a ghost before, so I was rather apprehensive. When I came up the stairs in the dark, with only a small flashlight to help me, I heard a sound that reminded me of a cat jumping from one landing to another. This was on the third-floor landing."

"Did you see a cat?" I asked.

"No, I didn't see a cat. I thought I was alone, that is, until I heard someone breathing in one of the rooms. Part of the floor was only rafters, without floorboards, so one could hear what went on on the floor below. It was one of the rooms on the second floor where the noise came from."

"What did the breathing sound like?"

"I thought I heard a man breathing rather heavily."

"What did you do next?"

"I was sitting up there on these rafters, and it was pretty dark. I didn't feel like meeting anyone, so I slept against a wall up there. I must have been asleep for a couple of hours. The wind was blowing, and I woke up once and went back to sleep again, and when I came to the second time it was just getting light. I went down and explored the house further and found the room where the noise had come from, and there was a sort of couch there, so I lay down for a bit and dozed off for another couple of hours. I looked at the room and realized that no one had slept there during the night."

Ruth Plant remarked at this point that the area where Mr. Armstrong had heard the heavy breathing was the same spot where her friend from Norway had also heard breathing, though she thought it could have been a woman, not necessarily a man.

Later on, the television people ran the controversial documentary for us. None of us saw the monk. We stopped action at the spot where thirty-one people said that they had seen the bearded monk, but all we could see were two men in conversation.

Nevertheless, the question of identifying the two ghosts at Morley intrigued me. This was one of the oldest and most fought-over spots in all of England, and the emotional imprint of many periods was undoubtedly still very strong. In antiquity the Iceni lived in this area. Their famous Queen Boadicea battled the Romans here in the first century. Later the Saxons made it a stronghold, and there is undoubtedly much undiscovered treasure in the ground. "A few years ago a ploughman turned up a wonderful collection of Saxon silver not far from Morley," Ruth Plant, ever the historian, explained. Scandinavian raiders had been there at an early stage: the word *mor* in Morley means mother in Norwegian. In 1066 a survey of all the land in England was undertaken. Known as the *Domesday Book*, it listed Morlea as belonging to one William de Warrenne. He was a wealthy Norman baron who took part in the Battle of Hastings. The *Domesday Book* also states that the land was let out to a priest and five freemen. Eventually the manor passed from the War-renne family into the hands of the Morleys, and in 1545 it was sold to Martin Sedley, a Roman Catholic, whose family held it until 1789, when the direct line died out. It appears that the house fell into disrepair soon after, for, according to Ruth Plant, the Norfolk Directory of 1836 describes it even then as a "farmhouse encom-passed by a deep moat." White's Norfolk Directory of 1864 named a certain Graber Brown as Lord of the Manor, and called Morley Old Hall "an Elizabethan house with a moat around it now used as a farmhouse." Eventually General Lord Ironside, World War I hero, bought it, but he passed on soon afterwards, and it passed into the hands of the Cotterills.

Since we could not stay on in Norfolk beyond the two days assigned to our visit, I entrusted further re-search to Ruth Plant. She concentrated on the monk and, whether through historical intuition or her psychic ability, shortly came up with some strange facts about one of the abbots of nearby Wyndmondham Abbey. "I unearthed the extraordinary fact that one of the abbots went completely mad and was so violent he was put into chains and died in them at Binham Priory. I be-lieve I can find out more about this if I go to St. Alban's Abbey where the records are kept."

I encouraged Ruth to undertake that journey, and a few months later she contacted me again.

Ruth had managed to get hold of a rare book in a London library which contained a commentary on the records of St. Alban's Abbey done by an eighteenth-century vicar. It contained the story of a prior of Wynd-mondham whose name was Alexander de Langley. "He went violently mad while in office at Wyndmondham and was recalled to St. Alban's," Ruth Plant informed me. "He lived around 1130 and died in chains at Binham Priory, about ten miles from Morley. I am sure Alexander de Langley, the mad prior, is the ghostly monk." In a further effort to throw light on the two ghosts at Morley, Ruth visited Lady Ironside, who resided at Hampton Court.

"I had agreed with Ricky Cotterill not to mention the ghostly side," Ruth Plant explained to me. "But she greeted me by remarking about 'that lovely Morley and the lovely lady who is seen standing at the window looking at the view.' She then asked me if I had ever visited it, making it quite clear she knew nothing of my psychic experiences concerning it. She added that many people have claimed to have seen her, though she didn't think that any of them would still be alive in the village to talk about it now."

But who *was* the ghostly lady at the window? Ruth Plant showed Lady Ironside the letters written to Anglia TV. One of the letters describes not a monk but a ghostly woman wearing a mantilla. Lady Ironside felt that the ghost must be Anne Shelton, daughter of one of the great supporters of Mary Tudor, which would account for the impression received by Ruth Plant that the female ghost was Catholic, and for her hearing a Hail Mary.

"As regards the monk, Lady Ironside told me that when they went there, Frank Warren's brother Guy, who farmed the place, told them, 'There is an old monk about the place, but you have no need to take any notice of him.' But she knew nothing about the coffin lid mentioned by Frank Warren."

Apparently, when Frank Warren was first being interviewed by Ruth Plant, he recalled Lord Ironside's coming out of the house one day carrying the stone lid of a coffin saying, "This belonged to a monk."

"But Lady Ironside mentioned that men, while excavating, had found a square stone with the name AL-BINI on it in Roman capitals. And since Wyndmondham was founded by Albini, the Norman baron who later became the Earl of Arundel and still later the Duke of Norfolk, the question is, was this the chapel of the Albinis, and was Morley a cell of Wyndmondham Abbey and of the Benedictine order?"

There you have it: a sixteenth-century Tudor lady, staying on forever in what was once her home, curiously looking out at a forever changing world; and a twelfth-century monk, gone mad, forced to die in chains ten miles from where he used to live. Perhaps he was drawn back to his house because it was there that he had committed his crime—killing a man, even if in self-defense, with a holy object as his weapon, thus compounding the crime. Was it the crime that had turned Alexander de Langley into a madman, or was it the madman in him that made him commit the crime?

7

THE GHOSTS
AT BLANCHLAND

The most obvious thing about Blanchland is its remoteness," writes G. W. O. Addleshaw in his short history of Blanchland. It wasn't as remote for us, because we arrived on a well-planned schedule, by private car, followed about two hours later by a busload of special tourists: participants in a Haunted Britain Tour arranged by Vision Travel, under the guidance of Andre Michalski, Polish nobleman and former orchestra conductor. Over the hills, into the dales, and over still another chain of hills we rode, shaken up all the while, but hopeful of eventually reaching our destination intact. By *we* I mean my wife Catherine and myself and London medium Trixie Allingham, whom I had invited to participate in a rare and unusual experiment. She hadn't the slightest idea why I was bringing her up north. All she knew was that I was on a ghost-hunting expedition, that she would have a quiet room that night and be brought back to London the following day.

When we left the airport at Newcastle, I had no idea that I would soon be in the heart of the Middle Ages, in a small market town so perfectly preserved that it gave one the impression of being in the middle of a motion-picture set in Hollywood. The square commons was reached through a city gate, turreted and fortified, and to the left was a solid-looking gray stone building with a colorful sign dangling from the second story. The sign read "Lord Crewe Arms." This was the unusual hotel which was once a sixteenth-century manor house, which in turn had been converted from a twelfth-century monastery.

The Abbey of Blanchland had been founded by Premonstratensian monks, a strict offshoot of the Benedictines. The land which gave the abbey its income was originally part of the old earldom of Northumbria, expropriated by Henry I for the Norman de Bolbec family. The family itself added some of their own lands in 1214, and it was then that the name Blanchland, which means white land, was mentioned for the first time. Most probably the name is derived from the white habits of the Premonstratensian monks. Up until the middle nineteenth century, the area around Blanchland was wild and desolate, very thinly populated and cut off from the outside world. This was, in a way, most fortunate, because it prevented Blanchland from being embroiled in the political struggles of the intervening centuries and allowed the monks to lead a more contemplative life here than in any other part of England. The monastery was dissolved under Henry

VIII, as were all others, and in 1539 the remaining monks were pensioned off, leaving Blanchland Abbey after four hundred years of residence. At first a family named Radcliffe owned the estates and buildings of the dissolved abbey, but in 1623 the Forsters, an old Northumberland family, came into possession of Blanchland. By now the church was in ruins, but a chapel still existed within the main building. Part of the abbey buildings were converted into houses for the village, and the abbot's residence became the manor house. When the last male of the line died, the property passed into the hands of Dorothy Forster, who had married Lord Crewe, Bishop of Durham.

When the owners of Blanchland got into financial difficulties in 1704, Lord Crewe bought the estates, and thus the name Crewe was linked with Blanchland from that moment on. Unfortunately for the family, they became embroiled in the Scottish rebellion of 1715, taking the Jacobite side. The estates eventually passed to a board of trustees, which rebuilt the damaged portion of the village.

A group of buildings, chiefly the kitchen and the prior's house, eventually became an unusual hotel, the Lord Crewe Arms, owned and operated by the Vaux Breweries of Sunderland. The stone-vaulted chamber of the house now serves as a bar. There is an outer stone staircase leading to the gateway and another one leading to what is called the Dorothy Forster Sitting Room, a room I was to know intimately.

We were welcomed by the manager, a Mr. Blenkinsopp, and shown to our quarters. Everything was furnished in eighteenth-century style. Our room, facing the rear, led onto a magnificent garden behind the house: obviously this was the monastery garden, or what remained of it. I understood from previous correspondence with the owner that the area is frequently plunged into sudden mists, but the day of our arrival was a particularly nice day in early August, and the sun was warm as late as seven o'clock at night. "Mrs. Holzer and yourself are in the Bambrugh Room," the manager said, with a significant raising of the eyebrows, when I came downstairs after unpacking. Then, making sure that no one was listening to our conversation, he added, "This is the room in which most of the activities are reputed to have taken place, you know." I nodded. I had specifically asked to be put up in the "haunted room."

Our arrival had gone unannounced, by my request; however, I offered to give a press interview *after* we had done our work. While my wife and Trixie rested after the journey from the airport, I took a walk around the premises. The peaceful atmosphere of the place was incredible. It almost belied the rumors of a haunting. A little later we had dinner in the candlelit bar downstairs. My psychic tour had meanwhile arrived and been placed in various rooms of the inn, and they were eager to participate in what for them was a unique and exciting adventure: to witness an actual seance or make contact with an authentic ghost!

It was already dark when we repaired to the room in which we were to sleep that night. Things were a bit on the tight side, with fourteen people trying to squeeze into a double bedroom. But we managed to find everyone a spot, and then Trixie took to a chair in one corner, closed her eyes and leaned back, waiting for the spirits to manifest.

Immediately Trixie looked up at me with a significant nod. "There was a murder in this room, you know," as if it were the most natural thing to expect from a room that was to serve as our sleeping quarters for the night.

"Anything else?" I said, preparing myself for the worst.

"I saw three monks come along, and the odd thing is one dropped his girdle—you know, the cord. It is all very odd."

I agreed that it was, but before I could ask her anything further, she pointed at the bed we were sitting on. "I see a woman lying on this bed, and she is dead. She has been murdered. This happened centuries ago. Now I see a little child running into the room, also wearing a dress of centuries ago. There is an unusual coffin leaving this room. I hear chanting. The coffin is black and shaped like a boat. I have the feeling this happened between the eleventh and thirteenth centuries. Also, I have a feeling of sword play and of a stone, a very special stone standing up somewhere outside."

At this point Trixie called for us to join hands to give her more power for what was to come.

Immediately her face became agitated, as if she were listening to something, something coming to her from far away. "I can hear somebody calling, 'Jesus, Jesus have mercy, Jesus have mercy,' and I see a monk wearing a dark habit, while the others are wearing a grayish white. But this man has on a dark robe which is extraordinary. He is a monk, yet he is really Satanic.

I think his name is Peter. I don't know whether he committed this murder or got caught up in it. He has a hawklike face, and there is a very beautiful woman who was tied to this monk. I hear her crying, 'Help me, help me, help me!' "

"How can we help her?" I asked.

"Get on your knees and pray," Trixie replied. "She wants absolution."

"What has she done?"

"*Credo, credo*—what does it mean?"

Trixie seemed puzzled, then she handed me a key. "Go to my room and you'll find a crucifix there. Bring it to me." I asked one of the tour members to get the crucifix from the room down the hall.

"This very beautiful girl died in childbirth, but it was not her husband's child," Trixie explained. "And now she wants absolution for what she has done. I hear 'Ave Maria.' She was buried stealthily outside this area, but she comes back here to visit this guilty love. Her progression is retarded because of her inability to clear her conscience, and yet one part of her wants to cling to the scene here. Wait a minute, I get 'Lord' something. Also, I wonder who was imprisoned for a time, because I see a jailer and rusty keys. It is all very much like looking at a movie screen—I'm getting bits and pieces of a picture. There is a great sense of remorse; this woman was married, yet she had this love for a monk. The child is lying on a bier. It is all tinged with murder. It seems she killed the child. Now I'm getting something about Spain and the Inquisition, but I don't understand why."

"Tell her she must divulge her name, so that she may be completely cleared," I suggested.

Trixie strained visibly to read the woman's name. "I get the initial F," she finally said.

"Can you get something about the period when this happened?"

"She said twelve hundred and sixty. She's beautiful; her hair is chestnut colored."

"What happened to the monk?"

"He was banished and died in misery, and she says, 'My fault, my fault!'"

I instructed Trixie to relieve the unhappy one of her guilt. Trixie took up the crucifix and intoned in a trembling voice, "You are forgiven and helped in Christ, the Savior!" I asked what was the name of the unlucky monk so that we could pray for him too. "F. F. F." Trixie replied. "He was a monsignor."

At this point, trance set in and Trixie turned more and more into the unhappy woman ghost. "I thought it would be some reparation for the misery I caused if I came back here. I am trying to impress my survival by coming from time to time. I do not see him now. Oh, we are separated from each other. I kneel in the church."

Trixie "returned," and the entity again spoke to her, with the medium relaying her messages to me. "When she was young, this house belonged to the earl." I offered to have some prayers said on her behalf in the church, but in whose name should they be said?

"Just pray for me. I shall know much happiness and I shall be free."

"Then go in peace with our blessings," I replied, and I could see that the entity was fast slipping away. Trixie came out of her psychic state now, visibly tired.

While she was recuperating, I asked the others whether they had felt anything peculiar during the seance. One lady spoke up and said that there was a sort of electric feeling in the room; another admitted to having a strong feeling that she received the impression of a monk who wasn't a real monk at all. Trixie said, "Now I understand about the three monks and one of them putting down his cord. He was being defrocked!"

Mr. Hewitt, one of the managers, had been present throughout the seance, watching with quiet interest. I asked him for verification of the material that had come through Trixie. "It all makes sense," he said, "but the peculiar thing is that the times are all mixed up—everything is correct, but there are two different layers of time involved."

The part of the building where the seance had taken place was the only part of the abbey remaining from the very early period, the Abbey of the White Monks—the white monks seen clairvoyantly by Trixie at the beginning of our session. Mr. Hewitt could not enlighten us concerning the defrocked monk, and when I mentioned it, Trixie filled me in on some of the details of her vision. "It was a terrible thing to see this monk. There he stood in his dark robe, then the cord dropped off and his habit came off, and then I saw him naked being flayed and flayed—it was a terrible thing."

According to the manager, several of the villagers have seen the apparition of a woman in the churchyard and also in the church next door to the hotel. People sleeping in the room we were in had at various times complained of a "presence," but nobody had actually seen her. "She was absolutely beautiful with her rust-colored hair," Trixie said. "I could just see her vaguely, but she had on a light dress, very low, nothing on her head, and her hair was loose." The manager turned to me and asked whether he might bring in a picture of the lady whom they suspected of being the ghost. When Trixie looked at it, she said firmly, "This is the girl I saw." The picture was a portrait of Dorothy Forster —Trixie had named the woman F.—and it was this Dorothy Forster who had played an important role in the history of Blanchland. In 1715, Dorothy's brother Thomas was a general in the Jacobite army, although he was not really qualified for the post. He was captured and imprisoned at Newgate Prison. Three days before his trial for high treason, his sister Dorothy managed to enter the prison, disguised as a servant, get her brother out, and help him escape to France, where he eventually died. Also of interest is the reference to the initials F. F. F. by Trixie. In 1701 a certain John Fenwick killed Ferdinando Forster in a duel at Newcastle. As a result of this, the estate fell into debt and was later sold to Lord Crewe, the Bishop of Durham. He in turn married Dorothy Forster's aunt, also named Dorothy. "There still seems to be some confusion as to which of the two Dorothys haunts the village and the hotel," says S. P. B. Mais in a pamphlet entitled "The Lord Crewe Arms, Blanchland." "She is to be seen walking along the Hexham Road and opens and shuts doors in the haunted wing of the hotel. A portrait of the niece hangs in the sitting room which is named after her, and a portrait of the aunt hangs in the dining room alongside that of her husband, the Bishop of Durham."

I realized by now that Trixie had tuned in on two

separate time layers: the grim twelfth and thirteenth centuries, together with the story of a monk who had done wrong and had been punished for it. This particular haunting or impression came as a surprise to the manager, because it had not been reported before. On the other hand, the ghostly presence of Dorothy Forster was generally known around the area. The question was, which Dorothy was the ghost? During the state bordering on trance, Trixie spoke of the house owned by the earl. This was in reply to the question of whose house it was when Dorothy was young. So the ghost could only be the niece, the second Dorothy, because Lord Crewe, the Bishop of Durham, had married her aunt, also named Dorothy. The younger Dorothy would have grown up in her aunt's house. But why was Dorothy Forster, the younger, seeking forgiveness of her sins? Here the mystery remains. On the one hand, Trixie identified the ghost from the portrait shown her by Mr. Hewitt; on the other hand, Dorothy Forster definitely had nothing to do with any monks, since in the eighteenth century there weren't any monks around Blanchland.

The following morning we left for Newcastle and a television interview. A reporter from one of the local papers, *The Northern Echo,* headlined the August 9, 1969, issue with "HAUNTED, YES—BUT WHOSE GHOST IS IT?"

Two psychic sisters from Dallas, Ceil Whitley and Jean Loupot, who had been on the haunted tour with us, decided to jot down their impressions in the haunted room immediately afterwards.

"Both of us feel that Trixie was mistaken in at least

one of her impressions. Trixie felt the young woman was inconsolable because she had killed her newborn child, but both of us had the definite impression that she said, 'did away with,' meaning, not killed. We thought it was spirited away by the monks who delivered it. We are so sure of this impression that we do want to go back to Blanchland and see if we can pick up anything further."

On September 15, 1970, the two ladies got in touch with me again. "When we were at Blanchland, Jean 'saw' a woman standing beside a wall at an open gateway. She was quite plump, approximately forty to forty-five years old, and dressed in a black, stiff, full-skirted, long-sleeved dress, nipped in at the waist. There was a laced scarf over her head, crossed in front and back over her shoulders. She stood with her arms crossed in front of her, and her face had a look of sad resignation, as though she were remembering some long-past sadness. We thought it was the girl we 'picked up' last summer, only she was showing us herself in middle age, though still suffering the loss of her child."

THE GHOSTS
OF EDINBURGH

I would not be so familiar with some of the ghosts in and around Edinburgh were it not for the friendship and enormous help given me by Elizabeth Byrd, the author of *Immortal Queen,* and Alanna Knight, author of *October Witch* and many other books, and her husband Alistair. These wonderful friends not only helped plan my recent visit to Scotland but spent much time with me as well. There is something very peculiar about the intellectual atmosphere of the Scottish capital: when you walk along the impressive eighteenth- and early nineteenth-century streets, you feel in the heart of things, yet also removed from the turbulence of the world.

"Guess what? I'm coming to Scotland," I wrote to Elizabeth in March of 1973. It was May 3 when I checked in at the George Hotel in the heart of Edinburgh. Shortly after my arrival, Elizabeth paid me a visit with detailed plans for the rest of my stay, pretty much in the manner of one of Napoleon's field marshals when the emperor was about to embark on a campaign. As my first official act on Scottish soil I presented Elizabeth with a large bottle of Scotch, imported from New York. Elizabeth had wanted to take me to one of the famous old hotels where she had had an uncanny experience in the ladies' room. There was some question on how to get me into the ladies' room and what to tell the manager. "Suppose I watched outside and barred any lady from coming in?" Elizabeth suggested. "Five minutes in there should suffice, should you feel any impression." I declined, explaining that I wouldn't mind going to a haunted men's room but then since there wasn't any at that particular hotel, I would pass. But my curiosity had been aroused, so I asked Elizabeth what exactly happened at the ladies' room at the ——— Hotel.

"Well," Elizabeth replied in her well-modulated voice, "last year on December 8, which happens to be my birthday, I was in a very happy mood. I was in Edinburgh for business appointments and to celebrate. At noon, I happened to run into a book dealer who invited me for a drink. So we went to the ——— Hotel. He ordered the drinks and I went upstairs to primp. The ladies' room is immaculate, new, and neon-lit. Absolutely nothing to frighten anyone, one would think. No one else was in there. I was there for about two minutes when a feeling of absolute terror came over me. Without so much as combing my hair, much less putting on lipstick, I just had to run."

"Did you hear or see anything?"

"No, just this feeling of terror. I went down two flights of stairs and was extremely glad to get that drink from the book dealer, who said, 'You look peculiar.' I kept wondering what had frightened me so. All I knew about the hotel was that it had been built around 1850. When I told a friend, Kenneth Macrae, what had happened to me in the ladies' room, he said, 'I know something about the history of the hotel.' He suggested I also check with *The Scotsman.*"

Elizabeth's greatest terror is fire, so she inquired whether there had been any disastrous fires at the hotel at any time. There had indeed been a fire in May of 1971 in which a woman was killed, and a chef had been found guilty of starting the fire and causing the woman's death. Earlier, in 1967, a fire had broken out in a club nearby and the hotel staff had been evacuated, but the fire had been quickly brought under control. The newspaper librarian regretted that there was no fire of any proportion at the hotel at any time. A little later Elizabeth went to London and while there she received a note from her friend Kenneth Macrae: "Dear Elizabeth, is it possible that your discomfort in the ladies' room was prophetic? A Welsh Rugby supporter was killed in a fire on February 3, 1973, in the hotel."

Miss Byrd thought that was the end of that, but then on April 29, 1973, a really disastrous fire broke out in the hotel, the result of which left two hundred people dead. "It must have been this really big fire I felt, long before it actually happened. I'm glad I wasn't in the hotel at that time."

But Alanna Knight had a different impression of

the haunted ladies' room. "Elizabeth insisted on taking me there one day. I must admit I was very skeptical, but as soon as I opened the door I got my unfailing signal —that old, familiar scalp-crawl—and I knew that despite the modern decor, and bright lights, there was something terribly wrong. Luckily we had the place to ourselves for the moment, although I must admit if Elizabeth had not been there, I would have taken to my heels at once!

"I felt immediately that she was mistaken about thinking it had anything to do with a fire. I got an impression of a woman, thirty-five to forty, sometime about 1910, who had suffered such a tragedy that she took her own life in that room. It was a particularly gruesome end, and the room absorbed it. My impression of her was that she was neat but rather shabbily dressed, a 'superior' servant, perhaps a housekeeper or a teacher or someone of that nature."

Because Elizabeth frequently visits the hotel where all this happened, she has asked I not give the hotel's name. She likes the bar, the dining room, and the lounge—everything, in fact, except the ladies' room. Therefore, when the call comes, there is but one thing for Elizabeth to do—leave.

The telephone rang. It was Ian Groat, who with his friend James Grandison, who would serve as the driver, was to take us to the outskirts of Edinburgh for a look at a haunted country house. During the ride from the center of town up into the hills surrounding it, I had an opportunity to interview Mr. Grandison.

"This happened in 1965, in a modern bungalow

built in 1935, on the outskirts of Edinburgh," he began in a soft voice colored by a pleasant Scottish burr. "The place was called Pendleton Gardens, and there had not been anything on the spot before. I lived there for about two years without experiencing anything out of the ordinary, but then strange things started to happen. At first we heard the sound of wood crackling in the fireplace, and when we checked, we found the fire hadn't been lit. Sometimes this noise would also occur in other parts of the place. Then there was the noise of dogs barking inside the house. My wife used to hear it on her own, and I of course discounted the whole thing, saying that there must have been a dog outside. But eventually I began to hear it as well. There were no dogs outside, and I was able to pinpoint the direction whence the bark came. Added to this was the noise of a kettle boiling over on a stove, as if one had to run to the kitchen and turn off the kettle. Whenever we approached the entrance to the kitchen, the noise stopped instantly. While we were still wondering about this, other things began to happen. A door would suddenly slam in our faces, just before we got to it. Or I would go to the bathroom, and the bathroom door would be halfway open, and just as I reached the handle, it would slam violently open, wide open."

"In other words, whoever was causing it was aware of you?"

"Oh, absolutely, yes. Then we started getting knocks on the walls. We tried to communicate by knocking back, and sure enough this thing kept knocking back at us, but we weren't able to establish a code, and apparently this thing didn't have enough energy to carry on indefinitely. We tried to ignore the whole thing, but then something or someone started to knock on the back door. Whenever we answered the door, there was no one there. One day I was lying on the bed while my wife Sadie was in another room with my mother. Suddenly I heard the sound of heavy footsteps walking down the path to the back door and someone knocking on the door. It sounded like a woman's footsteps, but I can't be sure. Then my wife and my mother also heard the footsteps going down the path. We did nothing about answering the door, and after a moment the noise came again, but this time it was a thunderous knock, *bang-bang-bang.* It sounded like someone was very annoyed at not getting in, and this time both my wife and my mother ran to open the door, and again there was no one there and no sound of footsteps receding up the path.

"We were in the habit of going away weekends then and coming back Sunday night. During our absence the house was well locked up, with safety locks on the windows and on the front door. The back door was barred entirely with bolts and quite impregnable; there was no way of getting in. The first time we did this, when we came back we found all sorts of things amiss: the hearth rug in the bedroom had been picked up neatly from the floor and placed in the center of the bed. An ashtray had been taken from the mantelpiece and put in the middle of the hearth rug. We had a loose carpet in the corridor running the length of the house. It was loose and not nailed down. After we got back from our weekend, we found this carpet neatly folded up end-to-end, and we had to unwind the thing again and put it back along the corridor. There was a large piece of wood in the living room, part of the back of a radio-phonograph. When we came back after the weekend, instead of lying against the wall, it was flat on the floor. So the following weekend, we put the piece of wood back against the wall and two chairs up against it so it couldn't possibly fall down. But when we came back, the wood was again right on the floor, yet the chairs had not been disturbed! Whoever it was who did it must have lifted it straight up over the chairs and slipped it out from behind them and placed it in the middle of the floor, as if they were saying, 'Look, I've done it again, even though you tried to stop me.' By now we were pretty sure we had a *poltergeist* in our house."

"What did you do about it?"

"While we were still trying to figure it out, there was an incident involving a cat. One day we clearly heard a cat purring in the middle of the kitchen floor. But our cat was sitting on a chair, looking down at this imaginary cat as if she could see it. We also heard a terrible crash in the living room, only to find nothing at all disturbed. Once in a while one would hear an odd note on the piano, an odd key being struck, but there was no one near it. This went on and on, gradually building up. At first it was perhaps one incident a week. Eventually it was happening every day. After two years it was getting really ridiculous, and we were beginning to worry in case the neighbors would hear dogs barking *inside* the house and things like that. Finally I asked a medium by the name of James Flanagan to come to the house."

"A professional medium?" I asked.

"It is a hobby with him, but he tells me that his work is his hobby, and the mediumship is his actual profession."

"What happened?"

"He brought another man with him, James Wright, and they had tape recorders with them. He informed us that he felt spirits all over the room, and that he could see them even though we couldn't. He told us it was the original owner of the house, an old lady; she had become strange and was put in a hospital, where she died. She didn't know that she was dead and insisted on coming back to her home. He described her as having reddish hair. Her husband had been a freemason."

"Did you check this out?"

"The person who had shown us round the house when we bought it," Mr. Grandison replied, "was a ginger-haired woman who turned out to have been the daughter of a lady who had died. Also we found a number of things in the attic having to do with freemasonry."

"What advice did the medium give you to get rid of the spook?"

"He asked us to get a basin of clean water and put it in the kitchen and to try to imagine his face in the basin of water after he had left. Also, in two weeks time the entire phenomenon would disappear—and much to our surprise, it did. Incidents were less frequent and eventually they ceased all together."

I had mentioned to Elizabeth Byrd that a certain David Reeves had been in touch with me concerning a *poltergeist* at his Edinburgh residence and expressed the desire to visit with Mr. Reeves.

"It all started at the beginning of 1970, when my cousin Gladys, her husband Richard, myself, and my wife Aileen were discussing the unknown and life after death," Mr. Reeves had stated to me. "We had heard of other people using a ouija board, so I drew one on a large piece of paper and placed it on the floor, then placed a tumbler in the center of the paper, and we all put our right forefingers on the glass. After a few minutes I experienced a cold shiver down my back and Richard said he felt the same. Then the glass started to move!"

They received no message, and Mr. Reeves was very skeptical about the whole thing. But the little circle continued using the ouija board, and eventually they did get evidential messages, from a spirit claiming to be Richard's grandfather. The message was succinct: Richard was to have a crash on his motorbike. A few weeks later he crashed his three-wheeler, which had a motorbike engine. Messages came to them now from different people. One night they received a message stating that the two men were to drink salt water(!) and to make their minds blank at precisely eleven o'clock.

"At eleven I 'fell asleep,' and what happened afterwards is an account told to me by the others," Mr. Reeves explained. In trance, through Mr. Reeves, an entity calling himself St. Francis of Assisi manifested. Since none of the group were Roman Catholics, this was rather surprising to them. The entranced David Reeves then got up, demanded that the light—which he called 'the false light'—be put out, and that the curtains be opened. This done, he demanded that everyone fall to his knees and pray. He himself then proceeded to pray in Latin, a language which neither Mr. Reeves nor any of those present knew.

Unfortunately, Mr. Reeves's cousin Gladys mistook his deep state of trance for illness and put the light on. Immediately he came out of his trance and complained of great pains in his hands.

"When I looked at them, they were covered by blood, and each hand had a hole in the center," Mr. Reeves said. "This was witnessed by everyone present. I quickly ran to the tap and washed the blood away. The holes then vanished."

But the holy tenor of their seances soon changed to something more earthy: Mr. Reeves was impressed with advance information concerning local horse racing and won quite a lot of money because of it. This was followed by what he described as a "distinct evil presence" in the circle, to the point where his wife refused to participate any longer. The other couple, Richard and Gladys, evidently took part of the presence to their own home: *poltergeistic* activities started and objects moved of their own volition. It was at this point that Mr. Reeves contacted me and wondered what they ought to do next. Unfortunately, I was unable to find him at the address he had given me. Had he been forced to move? I wrote him a note advising him to stay clear of ouija boards and to consider his experience in trance as a form of psychic hysteria: it could just be that a spirit who *wanted* to be St. Francis had taken over Mr. Reeves's body and expressed this unfulfilled desire for martyrdom.

The discussion of various ghostly events had made the time fly, and suddenly we halted at our destination, Woodhouse Lea. Ian Groat, a gunsmith by profession, had had an uncanny experience here and wanted me to see the place where it all happened. We were on a hill overlooking Edinburgh, and there were a stable and a modern house to our left. Farther up the hill, following the narrow road, one could make out the main house itself. According to my information, Woodhouse Lea had originally stood on another site, farther east, but had been transferred to the present spot. There was a local tradition of a "White Lady of Woodhouse Lea," and it was her appearance that I was after. It was a bitingly cold day for April, so we decided to stay in the car at first, while we sorted out Mr. Groat's experiences.

"In January of 1964 I went to Woodhouse Lea in the company of Mr. and Mrs. Peter London," Ian told us. "We waited for several hours in the basement of the house, which had been used to store fodder for horses."

"I gather you went there because of the tradition that a 'White Lady' appeared there?" I asked.

Ian nodded. "After about two hours, a fluorescent light appeared behind one of the doors, which was slightly ajar. It seemed to move backwards and forwards for about five minutes and then disappeared. All three of us saw it. The light was coming from behind that door. We were waiting to see whether anything would actually enter the room, but nothing did, and so we left."

"What was the house like at that point?"

"It was still standing, though several large pieces of

masonry had fallen and were lying in front of it. The woodwork was in very poor condition and floorboards were missing, but part of the original grand staircase was still there. It was dangerous to walk in it at night, and even in daylight one had to walk very carefully."

The house could have been restored, if someone had wanted to foot the expense. For a while the monument commission thought of doing it, but nothing came of it, and eventually the owners pulled it down. The decision was made in a hurry, almost as if to avoid publicity about the destruction of this historical landmark. It was all done in one weekend. The masonry and what was still standing was pulled to the ground by heavy machinery, then stamped into the ground to serve as a kind of base for the modern chalet which the owners of the land built on top of it. It reminded me of some of the barbarous practices going on in the United States in pulling down old landmarks in order to build something new and, preferably, profitable.

Peter London was shocked at the sudden disappearance of the old mansion house, and he got to talking to some of the girls working in the stables at the bottom of the hill, also part of the estate. Several of them had seen the apparition of a woman in white.

The strange thing is that the British army had invested seven thousand pounds in central heating equipment when they occupied the building. This was during World War II and the building was then still in pretty good shape.

"During the war there was a prisoner-of-war camp that bordered on the actual Woodhouse Lea Estate," Ian continued. "The sentries kept a log of events, and there are fourteen entries of interest, stretching over a three-year period. These concerned sightings of a 'woman in white' who was challenged by the sentries. Incidentally, the stable girls saw her walking about the grounds, *outside* the house, not in the house itself or in the stables."

I decided it was time to pay a visit to the area where the mansion last stood. Since there had been no time to make arrangements for my investigation, Mr. Groat went ahead, and to our pleasant surprise he returned quickly, asking us to come inside the stable office, at the bottom of the hill. There we were received by a jolly gentleman who introduced himself as Cedric Burton, manager of the estate. I explained the purpose of my visit. In Scotland, mentioning ghosts does not create any great stir: they consider it part of the natural phenomena of the area.

"As I know the story," Mr. Burton said, "her name was Lady Anne Bothwell, and originally she lived at the *old* Woodhouse Lea Castle, which is about four miles from here. Once when her husband was away, one of his enemies took over the castle and pushed her out, and she died in the snow. I gather she appears with nothing on at all when she does appear. That's the way she was pushed out—naked. Apparently her ghost makes such a nuisance of itself that the owners decided to move the castle and brought most of the stones over here and built the mansion house called Woodhouse Lea up on the hill. The last person I know of who heard a manifestation was a coachman named Sutherland, and that was just before electric light was installed. There has been no sign of her since."

"I gather there were a number of reports. What exactly did these people see?"

"Well, it was always the same door on the north side of the building, and on snowy nights there was a fairly vigorous knock on the door; and when someone would go outside to investigate, there was never anyone there—nor were there any footprints in the deep snow. That, I think, was the extent of the manifestations, which are of course tremendously exaggerated by the local people. Some say it is a White Lady, and one has even heard people coming up the drive. I've heard it said, when the old house was standing there empty, lights were seen in the rooms."

"Has the house ever been seriously investigated?"

"Some Edinburgh people asked permission and sat in the old house at midnight on midsummer's eve. However, I pointed out to them that she was only known to appear around seven in the evening and in deep snow. Midnight on midsummer's eve wasn't the most auspicious occasion to expect a manifestation. There was another chap who used to bring his dog up and stand there with his torch from time to time, to see if the dog was bristling."

"When did the actual event occur—the pushing out of the woman?"

"The house was moved to this spot in the early fifteenth century. It was originally built around the old Fulford Tower. It is a bit confusing, because up there also by the house there is an archway built from stones from an entirely different place with the date 1415 on it. This comes from the old Galaspas Hospital in Edinburgh."

"If Woodhouse Lea was moved from the original site to this hill in the early fifteenth century, when was the original house built?"

"Sometime during the Crusades, in the thirteenth century."

While the early history of Woodhouse Lea is shrouded in mystery, there was a Lord Woodhouse Lea in the eighteenth century, a well-known literary figure in Edinburgh. Many other literary figures stayed at the house, including Sir Walter Scott, Alan Ramsey, and James Hogg. Evidently Sir Walter Scott knew that *old* Woodhouse Lea was haunted, because he mentions it in one of his books, and Scottish travel books of the eighteenth century commonly refer to it as 'haunted Woodhouse Lea.' In 1932 control of the house passed into the hands of the army, and much damage was done to the structure. The army held onto it for thirty years.

"Have there been any manifestations reported in recent years?"

"Not really," Mr. Burton replied. "When the bulldozer pulled down the old house, we told people as a joke that the ghost would be trying to burrow her way out of the rubble. Some of the stones from the old house have been incorporated into the new chalet, built on top of the crushed masonry, to give it a sort of continuity."

The chalet is the property of George Buchanan Smith, whose family uses it as a holiday house. He is the son of Lord Balonough, and his younger brother is the undersecretary of state for foreign affairs in Scotland.

"The house has been talked about tremendously," Mr. Burton said. "It has even been described as the second most haunted house in Scotland. Also, Woseley is not too far from here, and it too has a nude white lady. She has been observed running on the battlements."

"Why did they move the house from the old site to this spot?"

"Because of her. She disturbed them too much."

"And did the manifestations continue on the new site?"

"Yes," Mr. Burton acknowledged. "She came with the stones."

He turned the office over to an assistant and took us up to the chalet. The owner was away, so there was no difficulty in walking about the house. It is a charmingly furnished modern weekend house, with a bit of ancient masonry incorporated into the walls here and there. I gazed at a particularly attractive stone frieze over the fireplace. Inscribed upon it, in Latin, were the words, OCCULTUS NON EXTINCTUS: the occult is not dead (just hidden).

9
LEITH HALL

When Elizabeth Byrd decided to forsake the United States for a residence in Scotland, I impressed on her the need to report any unusual hauntings to me so that in the event I should visit I'd have my work cut out for me. She was married at the time, and together with her husband she established residence in a wing of ancient Leith Hall in the central highlands of Scotland. The manor house belonged to a Scottish trust but in Great Britain old houses are often rented out to responsible tenants, and it is not as difficult to live in a castle as one would think. Shortly after getting settled at Leith Hall, which is not too far from the royal residence of Balmoral, Elizabeth went through a disturbing number of psychic experiences, some of which she has reported in her own book, *A Strange and Seeing Time*. Clearly, she was living in a haunted house. In the summer of 1969 I decided to pay Leith Hall a visit in the company of my Haunted Tour of Great Britain. The fifteen participants had a grand time: sleeping in private castles and getting to know real live lords and ladies, sometimes with upsetting results (for the lords and ladies, that is). They were in high spirits when the little bus we were using drew up in front of the Hall. Elizabeth's residence turned out to be a sturdy sixteenth-century Scottish manor house, fortified by round white towers in the four corners and rising to the height of three stories. It was well kept, and the part not used as apartments had been turned into a museum. Eventually we wound up in a lavish bedroom which had been Elizabeth's and her husband's.

"It was on July 16, 1968, last year," Elizabeth began, pointing at the bed. "I slept in this bed and was awakened at dawn by something or someone in the room. My husband was in London at the time, and I *knew* I was alone. It was quite bright, perhaps four or five in the morning, and the draperies were open. I stretched and turned and looked in that direction and thought, I know it's early, but I'll take the dog for a walk, so I started to get up. I turned in the direction of the window. There was a tall man there, standing in a commandlike stance. He had on very tight dark-green breeches and a pale-colored shirt. He had a beard and his head was bandaged—a dirty bandage—and I could scarcely see his eyes. I thought he was real, solid. There was no phosphorescence. First he stood there and then he sat on the bed. There was a weapon in his left hand, short and blunt."

"What did you do?"

"I screamed, 'Go away!' He hesitated and moved back a couple of steps. Then he went right through that mirror over there and vanished. I ran down the stairs to get the dog, as if for protection; then I came back and fainted. I woke up on top of the bed with the covers down at ten in the morning."

Immediately on awakening, Elizabeth telephoned her friend Alanna Knight, to report the apparition. When she had calmed down, Elizabeth tried to check on the identity of her ghost. She discovered in a book by Mrs. Leith-Hay, *Trusty to the End,* published in 1924, that a certain John Leith, who was the laird of Leith Hall, had left it and ridden to Aberdeen to have a 'merrie evening with gentlemen, at Campbell's Tavern. It appears that in the course of the evening John Leith got into an argument with a man named Abernathy. It is not clear whether a duel was fought or whether Abernathy simply murdered him, but Leith was shot through the head and his wound bandaged by his servant. He died three days later, Christmas Day.

In November of the same year, 1968, Elizabeth was away visiting Mrs. Knight in Aberdeen when her husband telephoned in great excitement and said, "I've just seen your bearded man." This time he was standing near the fireplace and again he looked quite solid. At first, Elizabeth's husband thought him to be an intruder.

"Did anyone else have an encounter with this ghost?" I asked. Elizabeth smiled at Alanna, who took up the narrative at this point.

"I slept in this bed on several occasions after Elizabeth was reluctant to stay," she explained. "My husband and I had come up to spend the night here. Independently, we both had nightmares of being suffocated. I didn't tell him about this at the time, because I thought it was just a nightmare, and my husband is a scientist and very skeptical. But we both had the same dream. Then in early January, my mother had also come up for a visit, and she slept upstairs, while my husband and I slept in this bed. Being elderly, my mother had never been told anything about Leith Hall, because she would be scared and reluctant to stay in a haunted house. She came down in the morning and said she had had the most peculiar experience. She had heard a pistol shot and then a sort of dragging sound like a man wearing heavy military boots walking along the corridor, blundering, and finally falling against the door. At this, she had sat up in bed and was very frightened. The sound went away, but then she heard the whole thing again about an hour later—blundering footsteps along the hall, and the bang at the door. During that same night, my husband woke up to the sound of shots being fired. Of course, there were no shots."

"Is it always a frightening experience?"

"Not necessarily," Mrs. Knight replied. "On another occasion when we stayed here, I awoke because I heard sounds of a meal being prepared. Not only that, but I smelled the food and I thought, Hmmm, Elizabeth and her husband are having a midnight feast somewhere! I sat up in bed and I thought, This is very odd! I could hear glasses, the clink of crystal, and the sound of cutlery, but I couldn't see anything at all. It was as if I were sitting at a table while a meal was being eaten around the table, *in this room*, just about at the foot of the bed. I could smell the food; I could hear the clink, the sort of mutter and rustling, and even laughter over there. It was completely dark, and it lasted about five minutes. Then it just faded away, and I thought, The people next door are having a dinner party. That was the only logical explanation."

At the time, Elizabeth and her husband were asleep upstairs, and there was no dinner party anywhere in the house.

Elizabeth broke in, "Alanna did not know at the time that this bedroom was once a dining room," she said. "The cupboard over there can be opened and it has an inscription, 'Best China.' When Lady Phyllis Borrough came here a while ago, she looked at the room and said, 'Oh, it is a bedroom now. It used to be a dining room—the dinner parties we had in this room!' Apparently the bathroom was a pantry, and food was brought up through some mechanical device."

We resumed our tour of the house. Most of it stemmed from the eighteenth century, but the older part goes back to the seventeenth century and was actually built on the site of Peel Castle, a much older house.

Alanna, a native of northern England, has lived with the occult all her life and considers it perfectly natural. Leith Hall particularly attracted her, and in some mysterious fashion has served as a catalyst for some strange flashbacks into earlier lives.

"The first time I stayed at the hall," Alanna said as we settled in Elizabeth's drawing room, "I slept in what Elizabeth called the haunted nursery up on the third floor. I woke up with a woman's face looking over me.

She said, 'Don't worry, dear, it will be all right.' I looked at her. She had on a dark, high-necked dress and I was conscious of sound outside the house, so I was sure I wasn't asleep. The strange woman had brown hair and blue eyes, long arms, and was rather striking looking."

Alanna saw her many times more at the Hall. Sometimes she would also look down on unusual scenes; there were times when she saw a dancing bear, and once she was taken to a stable and "saw" a newborn foal.

"I felt I was a child, perhaps of five years," she said, explaining her impressions of the past, "and I remember going out with a governess. She was holding me by the hand and there were other children with us who were running ahead. I must have been able to read a little, because I recognized the name Robert written on the front of a book, and I said something to the governess and she replied, 'No, you won't be able to read that, dear, until you're big.' There were no pictures in the book. Then I fell and grazed my knee, and she picked me up and carried me back. Then on another occasion I went to the stables and I described them to Elizabeth in every detail. At that time I had not explored the grounds of Leith Hall. Elizabeth confirmed that there was a place in the back, a coach house, which had always been kept locked. Finally, we managed to have it opened, and when I looked inside I realized that it was exactly what I had seen in my vision. *I had been there before.*"

"Were you ever able to pinpoint the exact time of this previous existence at Leith Hall?" I asked.

"Only yesterday I had one of those strange experiences," Alanna replied. "When I came here, I had the feeling as if I were going home, being drawn here. Frequently, I get the initial J. I see an old woman sitting in the bedroom with an emerald green bonnet, and I remember coming around the door and seeing her sitting there in a chair with a cane, sort of impatient. I've looked up the costume she wears in a book of designs and it seems to be around 1820."

"You're sure, then, that you've lived here before?" I asked her.

Alanna looked at me with a significant smile. "The very first time I slept here, in the old nursery, I said to Elizabeth: 'It's not like it used to be—it has more windows,' and Elizabeth went to ask one of the curators, a Miss Witt, about this, and she confirmed that the room used to be bigger but had been divided up. I also saw the front of the house without the big porch on it, and I saw myself as a little girl leaning out the window, and I heard my governess say, 'Now don't lean too far' and 'You mustn't catch cold' while I was watching a man with a dancing bear. Elizabeth confirmed that the porch had been put on much later. There is a lake on the grounds, but in my visions, I saw myself going to it with the governess, only it wasn't a lake at all, but rather a formal garden."

"I discovered that it had been a garden, but in 1904 it was turned into an artificial lake," Elizabeth Byrd added.

Alanna is convinced that she, Elizabeth, and others have shared an earlier lifetime at Leith Hall. A friend of Elizabeth Byrd, Carol Schowalter, stayed at Leith Hall in 1967. At the time, Alanna Knight knew nothing of her. When Elizabeth happened to show her a photograph of her friend Carol, Alanna blanched: it was the face of the governess she had seen in her dream visions!

On my return to New York, I decided to talk to Carol Schowalter. Carol had never had any psychic experiences before her visit to Leith Hall, nor did she know anything about the place prior to her visit there. She was given a small room next to where Alanna had slept, formerly part of one large room.

"The first thing I noticed were the very odd sounds: talking and laughing, people walking when you knew no people were there. Then eventually I began to feel their presence, too. It was all over the house. But the one room I seemed to have more reaction to than the others was what is now called the nursery, the big bedroom. My bedroom was right next to it. For almost four months, I would hear sounds in that room as if it were occupied. I would hear people turning over in bed, and one night I heard what sounded like someone falling out of bed, a very definite crash. There was no one anywhere near the room, and no furniture was displaced the next morning."

"Have you ever had the experience of feeling that you'd been to Leith Hall before you actually saw it?"

"No. The only feeling I had on the grounds outside the hall was on the coach-house road, which goes up to the very old stable. I was walking up with Elizabeth one day and suddenly had a very strong feeling that something bad, an accident or something of that type, had happened on this road."

I recalled Alanna Knight's testimony about the

governess and the child, and the visit to the stables, and I shuddered. Did she ever hear any voices?

"Definitely," she replied. "It was in the study used by Elizabeth's husband, and I was working with him, when suddenly we both heard a man's voice speaking to us. The man was obviously angry, but we couldn't quite make out the words. It is like when you hear someone in another room. It only lasted a few minutes, but it startled us so much that we both immediately ran to the only place where a man could have been, to see if he was there. There was no one.

"Sometimes the feeling of a presence was almost physical. Elizabeth and I were sitting together, talking about some happy subject. All of a sudden I knew there was someone else in the room. I then began to get a smothering feeling, like something was almost pressing on me. I felt very much in danger, as if something were enveloping me."

I recalled Alanna's testimony of being smothered, and her husband's account of a similar feeling.

"I told Elizabeth I had the feeling someone was trying to get into me, because I couldn't concentrate on what she was saying. I began to have an emotional anger, yet I wasn't angry at anyone. And then it passed. During that time, also, I had the distinct feeling that someone was standing right over the chair I was sitting in, threatening me with something. I remember once typing something for Elizabeth, and suddenly I realized I was the only person in the room—yet there were *two* people breathing!"

When Alanna heard I was coming to Scotland, she was delighted to serve not only as my guide but also as my medium, should that be required. "From our earliest days," Alanna explained, when we met for the first time, "I have inhabited two worlds, the daytime real one, and the dream world of sleep, with recognizable streets, houses, fields, roads, and of course people. Occasionally in reality I have visited places which have triggered remembrances of this dream world whence springs my feeling of *déjà vu*. When I was born I was so different in every way from my parents or relatives that I was regarded as an odd child, a changeling. From these whispered conversations grew my own childhood fantasies that I had been stolen not by, but *from* the Gypsies!"

Once, when Alanna was a teen-ager, she visited Holyrood Castle with her parents as part of a tour.

"As the guide was kind of long-winded and inclined to browse, I wandered out through a door in the cloisters and found myself in the grounds of the abbey. It was late summer, and, to my right, rolling lawns vanished into herbaceous borders and a stone wall circling the grounds. On my left, a high-railinged enclosure contained gravestones, with a locked gate, as if it were a private family burial ground. I followed the path along the railings, and just around the corner outside this burial place was a mound of grass, a grave with a crudely carved wooden marker and the words 'Dav. Rizzio' in large, sloping letters. I continued my walk in the empty garden, enjoying the sunshine, and returned the way I had come into the abbey, where I rejoined my parents and the tour. I never mentioned the grave because I always presumed that everyone *knew* it was there."

In the spring of 1971, Alanna was discussing Elizabeth's novel *Immortal Queen* with her, particularly a scene where Lord Darnley stumbles over Rizzio's grave in the grounds of Holyrood Abbey. Alanna informed Elizabeth that she had seen the grave. "Impossible," Elizabeth replied. "You couldn't have. No one knows where Rizzio is buried." Not satisfied with this explanation, Alanna asked an Edinburgh friend to check on it. Sure enough, the site of Rizzio's grave is still unknown. Rizzio was the Roman Catholic private secretary to Mary Queen of Scots, whom the Protestant lairds murdered in order to remove his influence on their Queen.

10

A VISIT WITH
ROBERT LOUIS STEVENSON

Helen Lillie Marwick is a newspaperwoman and writer who lives with her science-writer husband Charles in a delightful old house in Georgetown, Washington, D.C. It was on her insistence that I decided to pay a visit to the house once owned by Robert Louis Stevenson in Heriot Row, Edinburgh.

"A delightful Irish girl, Mrs. John Macfie, has bought the old Robert Louis Stevenson house and reports that the friendly ghost of R.L.S. himself has been around, and she hopes to keep him," Helen wrote.

I asked Alanna to arrange for a visit during my stay in Edinburgh, and on May 4, 1973, she and I arrived at the Stevenson House barely in time for tea. We had been asked for five o'clock, but our adventures in the countryside, on which I shall report in the next chapter, had caused us to be an hour late. It wasn't so much the

countryside as the enormous downpour which had accompanied this particular ghost hunt, and though it
gave it a certain aura, it created havoc with our schedule. But Kathleen Macfie shook hands with us as if we
were old friends and led us into the high-ceilinged
drawing room, one flight up. The large French windows allowed us to look out on what is probably one of
the finest streets in Edinburgh, and I could see at a
glance that Mrs. Macfie had refurbished the Stevenson
House in a manner that would have made Stevenson
feel right at home: a gentle blend of Victorian and
earlier furniture pieces and casual displays of artwork
in the manner of a home rather than a museum. Her
own strong vibrations, as the owner, filled the place
with an electrifying atmosphere of the kind that is so
very conducive to psychic occurrences. Our hostess
had blue eyes, red hair, and a direct practical approach
to everything, including ghosts. After we had had a
glass of sherry, she gave us the grand tour of the house.
It had been the home of Robert Louis Stevenson from
1857 to 1880.

"This was Mrs. Stevenson's domain," our hostess
explained. The magnificently furnished drawing room
was pretty much the way it must have been in Stevenson's day, except for the addition of electric light
and some of the personal belongings of the Macfies. In
particular, there was a chair by the window which Stevenson is said to have sat in when resting from his work.
As we walked in, I felt a distinct chill down my back,
and I knew it wasn't due to the weather. It was a definite touch of some sort. I asked Alanna whether she had
felt anything. She confirmed that she too had been

touched by unseen hands, *a very gentle kind of touch.* "I feel a presence. There is definitely someone here other than ourselves." I turned to Mrs. Macfie. "What exactly have you felt since you came to this house?"

"I am most sensitive to a feeling when I am alone in the house, but maybe that isn't right, because I never feel alone here. There is always somebody or something here, a friendly feeling. Actually, there are two people here. At first I thought, perhaps because of what I had read about Robert Louis Stevenson, I was imagining things. But then the Irish writer James Pope Hennessey came to stay with us. Mr. Hennessey had been to Vailina, on Samoa, where Robert Louis Stevenson lived and ended his days. There, in the South Seas, he had seen an apparition of Stevenson, and in this house he had seen it also. It happened in his own room because he slept back there in what we called the master bedroom."

"Have *you* seen anything?"

"No, but I feel it all the time. It is as though I would look around and there was somebody behind me. Sometimes, when I wake up early in the morning, especially in the winter, I feel as if there is somebody moving about. It is very difficult to talk about it. You see, my husband is an utter skeptic. He thinks it is the central heating. Even my small son would say, 'Oh, don't listen to Mother. She sees ghosts everywhere.' You see, the family doesn't support me at all."

Kathleen Macfie admits to having had similar "feelings" in other houses where she has lived. When she arrived at the Stevenson House eighteen months prior to our conversation, she soon realized that it was happening again.

"While the movers were still bringing the stuff in, I didn't pay any attention to what I felt or heard. I thought it was just the noise the movers were making. But then the feeling came: you know, when you are looking in a certain way you have peripheral vision and feelings; you don't have to look straight at anything to see it. You know that it is there. But it is a comforting, marvelous feeling."

Some of the poet's personal belongings were still in the house, intermingled with period pieces carefully chosen by the Macfies when they bought the house. "There is an invitation which he sent to his father's funeral, with his own signature on it," Mrs. Macfie commented. "But when his father died, his mother took nearly all the furniture out of here and went to live in Samoa with her son. When Stevenson himself died, the mother came back to Edinburgh to live with her sister, but Robert Louis Stevenson's widow brought all the furniture back to St. Helena, California, where she ended her days. By the way, this is his parents' room. His own room is up one flight. Originally the top story was only half a story, and it was for the servants, but Stevenson's parents wanted him to have proper accommodations up there, so that he could study and work. The house was built between 1790 and 1810. The Stevensons bought it from the original builders, because they wanted a house on drier ground."

Mrs. Macfie explained that she was in the process of turning part of the house into a private museum, so that people could pay homage to the place where Robert Louis Stevenson lived and did so much of his work.

We walked up to the second floor, Stevenson's own study. The room was filled with bookcases, and next to it was a bedroom, which Mr. Macfie uses as a dressing room. Nowadays there is a bed in the study, but in Stevenson's time there was no bed; just a large desk, a coal scuttle, and of course lots of books. I turned to Alanna and asked if she received any impressions from the room. She nodded.

"Near the fireplace I get an impression of *him*. When I just came in through the door it was as if somebody were there, standing beside the door."

While she was speaking, it seemed to me as if I, too, were being shown some sort of vague scene, something that sprang to my mind unexpectedly and most certainly not from my own unconscious. Rather than suppress it or attribute it to our discussion of Robert Louis Stevenson, of whom I knew very little at that point, I decided to "let it rip," saying whatever I felt and seeing if it could be sorted out to make some sense.

"Is there a person connected with this house wearing a rather dark coat and a light-colored or white shirtwaist type of thing with a small tie? He has rather dark eyes and his hair is brushed down. He has bushy eyebrows and he seems rather pale and agitated, and at this moment he is tearing up a letter."

Miss Macfie seemed amazed. "Yes, that is him exactly. His desk used to be where you're standing, and this was where his mother used to leave food for him on a little stool outside. She would come back hours later and it would still be there."

"I get something about age thirty-four," I said.

"Well, he was married then. On May 9, 1880, in fact." This was May 4, almost an anniversary.

We stepped into the adjacent room, which was

once Stevenson's bedroom. I asked Alanna whether she felt anything special. "The presence is much stronger here than in the other room," she said. Even while she was talking, I again had the strange urge to speak about something I knew nothing about.

"I have the impression of someone being desperately ill from a high fever and very lonely and near death. He's writing a letter to someone. He expects to die but survives nevertheless."

Both ladies nodded simultaneously. "During his teenage period, he was always desperately ill and never expected to survive," Alanna commented. "It was consumption, which today is called emphysema, an inflammation of the lungs."

Alanna Knight was eminently familiar with Robert Louis Stevenson, as she was working on a play about him. My knowledge of the great writer was confined to being aware of his name and what he had written, but I had not known anything about Stevenson's private life when I entered the house. Thus I allowed my own impressions to take the foreground, even though Alanna was far more qualified to delve into the psychic layer of the house.

"Was there any kind of religious conflict, a feeling of wanting to make up one's mind one way or the other? Is there any explanation of the feeling I had for his holding a crucifix and putting it down again, of being desperate, of going to consult with someone, of coming back and not knowing which way to turn?" I asked.

"This is absolutely accurate," Mrs. Macfie confirmed, "because he had a tremendous revulsion from the faith he had been brought up in, and this caused trouble with his father. He was Presbyterian, but he toyed with atheism and the theories of the early German philosophers. All of this created a terrible furor with his father."

"Another thing just went through my mind: was he at any time interested in becoming a doctor, or was there a doctor in the family?"

"He was trained as a lawyer, very reluctantly," Mrs. Macfie replied; "his father wanted him to become an engineer. But because of his uncertain health he never practiced law. His uncle, Dr. Louis Balfour, insisted that he leave Edinburgh for his health. His wife, Fannie Osborne, was very interested in medicine; she helped keep him alive."

Alanna seemed puzzled by something she "received" at this moment. "Was there a dog of a very special breed, a very elegant dog? When he died, was there great upheaval because of it? I feel that there was a very strong attachment to this dog." Mrs. Macfie beamed at this. "There was a West Highland terrier that he took all over. The dog's name was Rogue and he was very attached to it."

We thanked our hostess and prepared to leave the house. It was almost dinnertime and the rain outside had stopped. As we opened the heavy door to walk out into Heriot Row, I looked back at Kathleen Macfie, standing on the first-floor landing smiling at us. Her husband had just returned and after a polite introduction excused himself to go upstairs to his room—formerly Robert Louis Stevenson's study and bedroom. Except for him and for Mrs. Macfie on the first-floor landing, the house was empty at this moment. Or was it? I looked back into the hallway and had the distinct impression of a dark-eyed man standing there, looking at us with curiosity, not sure whether he should come forward or stay in the shadows. But it probably was only my imagination.

11

THE GHOSTLY
MONK OF MONKTON

When Elizabeth Byrd moved into a monastic tower at Old Craig Hall at Musselburgh nine miles outside of Edinburgh, she probably didn't figure on sharing the quarters with a ghost, much less a monk. If there is one thing Elizabeth Byrd doesn't want to share quarters with, it is a monk. As for ghosts, she has an open mind: to begin with, she has had ghostly experiences all through the years.

The monastic tower has two stories and is part of a larger complex of buildings which was once a monastery. Her landlord, who is also a good friend, lives in the main house, while Elizabeth is lady of the manor, so to speak, in her tower—an ideal situation for a romantically inclined writer, and she has been able to turn out several novels since moving into Monkton, as the place is called.

We had left my visit to Monkton for the evening of my second day in Edinburgh, and it turned out to be a foggy, chilly day. Alistair and Alanna Knight brought me in their car, and Ian Groat, the gunsmith whom I had met earlier, was also there.

One walks up a winding stair from the ground floor to the main floor, in which Elizabeth has made her home. The apartment consists of a living room with fireplace, a small kitchen and pantry to one side, and a bedroom to the other. I am sure that when the monks had the place, they did not do nearly so well as Elizabeth does now, so I can readily understand why a monk, especially a ghostly monk, would be attracted to the situation. We grouped ourselves around the fireplace with only a candle illuminating the room.

"I rented this cottage in February, 1972," Elizabeth Byrd began the account of her experiences. "I found it beautifully peaceful and benign. I discovered that the cottage was built in 1459, across a courtyard from a fortified house, which goes back to the twelfth century. Not much is known about my cottage except that it was built by monks. They worked this as an agricultural area, and it was an extension of Newbattle Abbey near Dalkeith. It came to be called 'The Town of the Monks.' From this, the name Monkton developed."

"During the year and a quarter that you have lived here," I said, "have you had any unusual experiences?"

"Yes," Elizabeth replied. "Six months after I got here I was reading in bed one night with the light on when I smelled a marvelous juicy kind of baking of meat, or the roasting of meat, which seemed to emanate from the old stone fireplace. It actually made me hungry. Of course I wasn't doing any cooking. This happened three or four times in the subsequent weeks, but I took it in stride, just looked up from my book and said to myself, 'Oh, there it is again, that smell.' It wasn't the kind of meat that you get in the supermarket: it was more like standing rib roast—expensive, gorgeous meat."

Alanna took up the narrative at this point. "I stayed at this cottage about a year ago for the first time. Of course, I was rather apprehensive of what I might find, but I found nothing but this wonderful feeling of great happiness and content. The first time I stayed here with Alistair, we went off to bed and slept in Elizabeth's room, and she slept in her study; it was a Saturday night. I woke up early Sunday morning and there was the sound of bells ringing. It must have been about six o'clock in the morning and I thought, 'Ah, there must be a Catholic church somewhere nearby. This is obviously a call to early Mass.' So I didn't wake my husband, but soon I heard the sound of trotting horses, and again I thought, 'Oh, well, that is somebody out with their horses. After all it is in the country.' When we had breakfast, I asked my husband whether the sound of the bells didn't wake him around six o'clock. He said, 'What bells?' I didn't say anything, but when Elizabeth came in I asked her, 'Doesn't the bell wake you up on a Sunday morning? Where is your church near here?' She said, 'We don't have a church here.' Actually, the bell I heard was on the side of the house."

"The bell has never been heard by anyone except by Alanna. There is no church within miles," Elizabeth said.

"Last March I stayed here again," Alanna continued. "I slept in Elizabeth's room, and around eight in the morning I woke up to a wonderful smell of food and thought. 'Oh, good, Elizabeth is making something absolutely delicious for breakfast,' and it was the most gorgeous, juicy smell, a gamey smell. There was also the smell of lovely, fresh bread. I jumped out of bed and rushed into the kitchen. There was no sign of Elizabeth and nothing was cooking. It was all emanating from the bedroom."

Now it was Ian Groat's turn.

"In January, 1973, I was asked to spend a few days' holiday here. On the first night I retired about four-thirty. Before falling asleep, I realized that I might see things, not because Elizabeth had told me of anything in particular, but because I suspected there was a good reason why she wanted me to sleep in this particular room."

"Did you, in fact, see anything unusual?"

"Yes," the gunsmith replied. "The first thing I saw was a trap door slightly to the left, in the floor, and a pair of steps leading to the basement. I saw the top of the trap door and a small monk appeared and looked at me. He had climbed the steps into the bedroom and was looking around, but he didn't seem to see me. Since he didn't see me at all, I allowed myself to relax completely. Then I saw a procession come in. One appeared to be a high dignitary of the Roman Catholic Church. He may have been a bishop. He was flanked by monks and they seemed to be chanting. I had a very good look at the bishop. He was clean-shaven, with a very serene face, and he looked very intelligent. The procession walked past me and more or less disappeared.

"Now another apparition appeared which caused me a great deal of confusion. I had decided I could see through the floor if I cared to exercise my faculty to do so. So I looked through the floor, and what I saw were bales of hay, and then I saw what appeared to be an opening in the wall, and through it came what I took to be either Vikings or Saxons. They were dressed in rough clothing. There were three of them—an old man, bearded, with gray hair, and two others, younger and fair-haired, also bearded, and none of them had weapons. I thought them to be farmers. They came through this cavity in the wall and they raised their hands in a greeting sign, but not at me. I was more or less an observer. Then I decided, since I could see through the floor, that I could perhaps see outside the building as well, and I then viewed the building from a height. Now I appeared to be on a parallel which was outside this dwelling, looking down. I saw soldiers coming up the drive and around the corner, and they seemed to be of the middle seventeen hundreds, dressed in gray coats of a very superior material. The accoutrements seemed to be made of white webbing. They were playing their drums and keeping step with them as they marched. I gained the impression that I was seeing this standing in a tower, but there is no tower there. I tried to see more, but I didn't, so I decided to go to sleep."

"My landlord, John Calderwood Miller," Elizabeth Byrd added, "bought this property in 1956 and restored it. There is a reference to it in Nigel Trentor's book, *The Fortified House in Scotland.* I told Mr. Miller about Ian's experience of having seen the hole in the floor and the monk going down and the hay, and he said, 'That is extraordinary, because in 1956 there *was* a hole in the floor between where your beds are now, and we had to cover it over and make a floor.' There was an exit down to what had been the stables where there were indeed horses. Now it is a garage and sheds."

There was still another witness to the haunting at Monkton: Ian Adam, whom I had interviewed in London, the mediumistic gentleman who had been so helpful to me during my ghost-hunting expedition in April. Originally of Scottish background, Ian liked coming up to Edinburgh. The morning of December 27, 1972, he arrived at three forty-five. Elizabeth Byrd remembers it clearly; not too many of her friends drop in at that hour. But he was driving up from Newcastle with a friend, and Elizabeth had gotten worried.

"It was a very cold night, and Elizabeth greeted us as only Elizabeth can," Ian told me. "Immediately we sat down in her sitting room, she asked, 'Do you feel anything here?' but even before she had said it, I had felt that it had a very peaceful atmosphere about it."

"Within ten minutes, out of the blue, Ian, who had never been here, said, 'What a strong scent of rosemary! This place is redolent of rosemary!'" Elizabeth reported Ian as exclaiming, but none of the others could smell it.

"The place was very lovely, really," Ian said, "and I told Elizabeth I was sure there was a woman there, a very industrious lady, perhaps of the fifteenth century. She appeared to me to be wearing a sort of off-white dress and was very busy cooking, as if she had an enormous amount of work to do. She seemed young, and yet old for her years, probably owing to hard work. There was a definite sense of tremendous activity about her, as if she had an awful lot of people to look after. I had a strong feeling that the place was one of healing. I saw a man sitting in a corner on a chair; his leg was being dressed and strapped, and he was being given an old-fashioned jug, or bottle, to drink from by another man. I think it had an anesthetic in it. I remember distinctly there was a great deal of good being done in this place, as if it were a place where people came for shelter and healing, if there were accidents or fighting. It was certainly a place of great spiritual power."

When I checked Ian's testimony with Elizabeth, who had written down his impressions immediately after he had given them to her, she changed the description of the woman ghost somewhat. According to Elizabeth's notes, the woman seemed between thirty and forty years of age, wearing pale gray, sort of looped up on one side.

"Was the impression of the man being helped and of the woman doing the cooking simply an imprint of the past, or do you think these were ghosts that you saw?"

"Oh," Ian said firmly, "they were ghosts all right." He couldn't hear anything, but he did smell the cooking.

"Did anything else happen during that night?"

"No. I had a very peaceful night, although I was absolutely freezing. It must have been the coldest night I've ever lived through. In fact, I got out of bed in the middle of the night and put a jersey over my head to protect myself from the intense cold."

There is one more witness to the haunting at Monkton. James Boyd, by profession a sales representative, but gifted with psychic and healing powers, once stayed overnight in the same bedroom Ian Groat slept in when he had his remarkable experience. This was in early April of 1972.

"In the morning he came to me," Elizabeth said, "and reported that there was a woman in a long, dirty-white dress who seemed to be very busy about the fireplace in the bedroom. The two fireplaces in the sitting room, where we are now, and the bedroom next door, were once connected. James Boyd also told me, 'She's very busy and tired because she works so hard.' He had, of course, no knowledge of Ian Adam's experience in the house."

Ian Groat spoke up now. "Two weeks after his visit here, James Boyd telephoned me and said, 'Ian, I have the feeling that there is a well in that courtyard. It is all covered up, but I think if you go down that well, about halfway down, you will find a cavity in the wall and in this cavity lots of silver, household silver that was hidden in times of danger.' I promised I would tell Elizabeth about it and I did."

"There is indeed such a well in the courtyard," Elizabeth confirmed, "but the tower that Ian Groat mentioned no longer exists. It was part of a peel tower, used for defense. When I told Mr. Miller about the well, he said, 'Now that is very extraordinary. About a year ago I went down into the well, about fifteen feet, and when I looked up, the light seemed far away.' Mr. Miller decided to go back up, as he didn't know what he might hit down in the depths. But he did have the feeling that there was a treasure somewhere and encouraged me and my friends to look for it."

Now that everyone had had his say, it was time to tell them of my own impressions. While the others were talking about the bedroom, I had the very distinct impression of a large, rather heavy monk watching from the doorway. He had on a grayish kind of robe, and there was a rather quizzical expression on his face, as if he were studying us. The name Nicholas rushed at me. I also had the feeling that there was some agricultural activity going on around here, with chickens and geese and supplies, and that in some way the military were involved with these supplies. These impressions came to me *before* the others had given their respective testimonies.

"The monk I saw had a gray robe on," Ian Groat confirmed, "and my impression was that I was seeing events that had occurred and not people who were present at that particular moment. It was like seeing a film from the past."

Well, if the monks and the lady at Elizabeth's Monkton Tower are film actors, they are one step ahead of Hollywood: you can actually *smell* the food!

12

SCOTTISH COUNTRY GHOSTS

For a day in early May, the morning certainly looked peculiar: heavy, moist fog was covering most of Edinburgh; fires were burning in all the fireplaces of the hotel; and the electric light had to be turned on at nine in the morning. It didn't seem to bother the natives much, not even when the fog gave way to heavy rain of the kind I know so well from the Austrian mountains. Just the same, a schedule is a schedule. Promptly at ten Alistair and Alanna Knight called for me at the Hotel George, and we embarked on the trip we had planned well in advance. Alistair was well armed with maps of the area to the south and east of Edinburgh, to make sure that we did not lose time in going off on the wrong road. Since the Knights came from Aberdeen, they were not so familiar with the countryside farther south as native Edinburghers might be, and the whole trip took on even more the mood of an adventure. At first we followed one of the main roads leading out of town, but when we got on top of a steep hill in the southeastern suburbs of Edinburgh, the fog returned and enveloped us so thoroughly that Alistair had to halt the car. We decided to trust our intuition, and between Alanna and myself, we put our ESP to work, such as it was, telling Alistair to go straight until he came to a certain side road, which he was to take. To our immense relief, the fog lifted just then and we discovered that we had been on the right road all along.

It all started with a note from Mrs. Agnes Cheyne, who wanted to tell me about an unusual spot eight miles from Edinburgh called Auchindinny, Midlothian. "I was born there in 1898," Mrs. Cheyne had written. "I am no chicken." The ghost who haunts the "Firth Woods" is that of a woman who was jilted by her lover and in great distress jumped from a great height into the river Esh. That, at least, is the tradition. Mrs. Cheyne's aunt, who wasn't convinced of the reality of ghosts, happened to be walking through an abandoned railroad tunnel running through to Dalmor Mill. At the mill, there are two old railroad tunnels left over from a branch of the Edinburgh railroad which has long been abandoned for lack of business. The tracks of course were taken up many years ago, but the tunnels have remained as a silent testimony to the colorful era of railroading. Today, the mill uses the road and trucks to do business with the outside world. It is a quiet, wooded part of the country, very much off the beaten track both to tourists and to business people, and it has retained much of the original charm it must have had throughout the nineteenth century.

The lady walked into the tunnel, and when she came to the middle of it, she suddenly froze in terror. There was a woman coming toward her, seemingly out of nowhere. Her clothes showed her to be from an earlier period, and there were no sounds to her footsteps. Mrs. Cheyne's aunt looked closer, and suddenly the apparition disappeared before her eyes. Although she had never believed in ghosts, that day she returned home to Edinburgh in a very shaken condition.

After about forty-five minutes, we reached a narrow country road, and despite the heavy rain, we managed to see a sign reading "Dalmor Mill." A few moments later, a branch road descended toward the river bank, and there was the mill. We ignored a sign warning trespassers not to park their cars and looked around. There was a tunnel to the right and one to the left. First we investigated the one on the right. Inside, everything was dry, and I remarked what wonderful mushrooms one could grow in it. We had scarcely walked ten yards when Alanna turned back, saying, "This is not the right tunnel. Let's try the other one." As soon as we had walked into the second tunnel, all of us felt an icy atmosphere which was far in excess of what the rainy day would bring about. Besides, the first tunnel was not equally cold. When we reached the middle of the tunnel Alanna stopped. "I wouldn't want to walk through this at night," she said, "and even in the daytime I wouldn't walk through it *alone.*"

"What do you feel here?" I asked. I had not told the Knights about Mrs. Cheyne's letter or why we were here.

"There is something about the middle of this tunnel that is very frightening. I have a feeling of absolute panic, and this started when I was halfway through this tunnel." Without further ado, Alanna turned back and sat in the car. I am sure that no amount of persuasion could have gotten her back into that tunnel again.

Twenty-three miles from Edinburgh, in a fertile valley that was once the center of the mill industry but is now largely agricultural, there stands the town of Peebles. The surrounding countryside is known as Peebleshire and there are a number of lovely vacation spots in the area, quiet conservative villas and small hotels much favored by the English and the Scottish. One such hotel is the Venlaw Castle Hotel, standing on a bluff on the outskirts of town, seven hundred feet above sea level. It is open for summer guests only and does indeed give the appearance of a castle from the outside. Standing four stories high, with a round tower in one corner, Venlaw Castle represents the fortified house of Scotland rather than the heavy, medieval fortress. Access to the castle, now the hotel, is from the rear; behind it, Venlaw, the hill which gave it its name, rises still further. The present building was erected in 1782 on the site of an old Scottish keep called Smithfield Castle, one of the strong points of the borderland in olden days. One half of the present house was added in 1854, in what is locally known as the mock baronial style.

Venlaw belonged to the Erskine family and in 1914 Lady Erskine offered her mansion to the admiralty as a convalescent hospital for twelve naval officers. According to James Walter Buchanan's *A History of Peebleshire*, it remained an auxiliary Red Cross hospital to the end of World War I. The same author describes the

present dwelling house as being "built on a command-
ing position with one of the finest views in the county.
It is presumed that it occupies the site of the ancient
castle of Smithfield, which was in existence until about
the middle of the eighteenth century."

In 1949 the house passed into the hands of Alexander Cumming, the father of the present owner, who
turned it into a small hotel.

In the summer of 1968 an American couple, Mr.
and Mrs. Joseph Senitt, decided to spend a few days at
Venlaw Castle. "The room we occupied was at the end
of the middle floor with a little turret room which my
daughter used," Mrs. Senitt had explained to me. "The
very first night we were there, the room was ice cold
even though it was July, and we couldn't wait to close
the lights and go to sleep. Immediately upon getting
into bed, I suddenly heard a long-drawn-out and quite
human sigh! It seemed to be near the foot of my bed.
For the moment I froze—I was afraid to move or even
breathe. If it hadn't been for the fact that my husband
was with me, I might have gone into shock. I said nothing to him, as he usually kids me about my ghostly
beliefs, and I felt he was probably asleep, as he made no
move and said nothing. However, after a moment I got
the strongest feeling that if it was a ghost it was friendly,
because I felt welcome."

When the Senitts left the castle a few days later,
Mrs. Senitt finally mentioned the incident to her husband. To her surprise he confirmed that he too had
heard the sound. He had attributed it to their daughter,
sleeping in the small room next door. But Mrs. Senitt
was sure that the sound came from in front of her, and

the turret bedroom where the girl slept was off to a corner in back of the room and the door was closed. Also, the Senitts were the only people staying in that part of the hotel at the time.

It was still raining when we crossed the river Tweed and headed into Peebles. The castle-hotel was easy to find, and a few minutes later we arrived in front of it, wondering whether it would be open, since we had not been able to announce our coming. To our pleasant surprise a soft-spoken young man bade us welcome, and it turned out that he was the owner, the son of the man who had opened the hotel originally, and also that he was the only person in the hotel at the present time, since it was not yet open for the season. I asked him to show us the room on the middle floor with the turret bedroom without, however, indicating my reasons for this request. I merely mentioned that some American friends of mine had enjoyed their stay at Venlaw, and I wanted to see the room they'd occupied. As soon as we had entered the room, Alanna turned to me and said, "There is something here. I'm getting a cold, crawly scalp." While Alanna was getting her psychic bearings, I took Mr. Cumming aside, out of her earshot, and questioned him about the hotel. Was there, to his recollection, any incident connected with the house, either since it had been turned into a hotel or before, involving death or tragedy or anything unusual?

Mr. Cumming seemed a bit uneasy at this question. "There are things we don't like to speak about," he finally said. "We've only had one traumatic accident. About twenty years ago one of our guests fell from a bedroom window."

Alanna came over at this point and stopped short of the window. "There's something at this window," she said. "Somebody either threw himself out of this window or fell out." But Alanna insisted that the tragedy went back a long time, which puzzled me. Was she confusing her time periods, or did a second death follow an earlier death, perhaps caused by a possessing entity? Those are the kinds of thoughts that race through a psychic investigator's mind at a time like this. Actually, it turned out that the guest fell out of a window one flight higher than the room we were in. He was a miner who had become ill and somehow fallen out the window. His friends carried him back in, but he had a broken neck; they actually killed him by moving him.

Alanna shook her head. "No. What I feel has to do with this window in this room. It may have something to do with the original place that stood here before. I get the feeling of a fire."

"Well," Mr. Cumming said, "Venlaw Hill, where we are standing, was the place where, during the persecutions, witches were burned, or people accused of such."

"I have feelings of intense suffering," Alanna said, "and I sense some noise, the feeling of noise and of a great deal of confusion and excitement. I get the feeling of a crowd of people, and of anger. Someone either fell out of this window or was thrown out, and also there is a feeling of fire. But this is definitely a woman. I feel it not only in this room but down on this terrace below, which seems to have something to do with it."

I questioned Mr. Cumming whether any of his guests had ever complained about unusual phenomena.

"Not really," he replied. "We did have a guest who complained of noises, but she was mentally disturbed. She was a resident here for some time in the 1950's. I didn't know her well; I was very young at the time."

"And where did this lady stay?" I asked.

"Why, come to think of it, in the room next to this one."

I thanked Mr. Cumming and wondered whether the lady guest had really been unhinged, or whether perhaps she had only felt what Mr. and Mrs. Senitt felt some fifteen years later in the same area.

The afternoon was still young, and we had two hours left to explore the countryside. We decided to cross the river Tweed once again and make for Traquair House, making sure, however, to telephone ahead, since this was not one of the days on which this private manor house could be visited.

Known as the "oldest inhabited house in Scotland," Traquair House at Innerleithen rises to five stories amid a majestic park, in a tranquil setting that gives the illusion of another century, another world. It is now owned by Lord Maxwell Stuart, of a distinguished noble family, related to the royal Stuarts. There is a tradition that the magnificent gates of Traquair, surmounted by fabled animals, shall remain closed until a Stuart king is crowned again in London. This Jacobite sentiment goes back to the times when the earls of Traquair gave support to the Stuart cause, but the present laird, Peter Maxwell Stuart, is more concerned with the quality of the beer he brews. He's also the author of a magnificently illustrated booklet detailing the treasures at Traquair House. These include, in the king's room, the bed in which Mary Queen of Scots slept, with a coverlet made by her ladies in waiting. That she slept there is not surprising, since Lady Mary Seaton, the wife of the second earl, was one of Mary's favorite ladies in waiting. Also, the very cradle used by Mary Stuart for her son James VI of Scotland now stands at Traquair, and in the many rooms of the house there are displayed treasures, documents, arms, and fine furniture, all of them dating back to the sixteenth and seventeenth centuries, when this great house was at its zenith. Much as we loved the sight of this beautiful house, so romantic on a rainy day, with the fog just lifting, we had come not to admire the antiques but to find out about its ghosts.

The caretaker, Andrew Aiken Burns, who had been at the house since 1934, took us around, painstakingly explaining room after room.

"Have you ever had any psychic experiences here?"

"Yes," he nodded, as if it were the most natural thing in the world to be asked. "It happened in 1936 in the afternoon of a beautiful summer day. I was out with my horse, clearing the brush from the front of the house, near the old ruined cottage in the field. My horse was a chestnut named Ginger, and suddenly he flicked his ears and I looked up. I saw a lady coming down the grass, dressed in a Victorian dress. She walked slowly down through the gate and into the cottage and then through the wicket gate into the garden."

"What was so special about that? Could she not have been a visitor?" I asked.

"Well, I left my horse and went right up to see where this person had gone, and the wicket gate was shut. She had been through the gate, and still the gate was shut."

"Did you ever see her again?"

"No. But later someone showed me some old photographs, and I recognized one as the lady I had seen walking on the grass. It was Lady Louisa Stuart."

Lady Louisa Stuart died in 1875 at age one hundred. She is buried in a vault in the Traquair churchyard, right in back of the castle. Why would she walk the grounds? I wondered.

According to the twentieth laird, Traquair House goes back to the tenth century when a heather hut stood on the place. In 1107 King Alexander I granted a charter to the Traquairs, and he was the first of a long line of Scottish kings who stayed here. Incidentally, Traquair means dwelling on a winding river. In the thirteenth century the building was incorporated into a border peel, a defensive palisade, and it served as such during the long period of border strife. In 1491 James Stuart, the son of the Earl of Buchan, became the first Laird of Traquair, and from him the present family is descended. Over the centuries the building was largely altered and added to, to fit the changing times. What was once an austere border fortress became a Renaissance castle and eventually one of the finer residences in Scotland. During the Civil War in the seventeenth century, Traquair became what the present laird describes as, "one of the great bastions of the Catholic faith in Scotland," because of marriages with Catholic ladies. Since Catholicism was not favored in this part of the country, Mass had to be celebrated in secret. To this day, there is a Roman Catholic chapel on the grounds, unfortunately decorated in the most gaudy modern style and totally at variance with the rest of the house. In 1688 the house was raided by a mob from Peebles, and all the religious articles found were destroyed. It wasn't until well into the nineteenth century that Catholicism was freely admitted into Scotland. During the rebellion of 1715, Traquair sided with Bonnie Prince Charles, which brought much misfortune upon the family.

When Charles Stuart, the fourteenth laird, died unmarried in 1861, the property passed into the hands of his sister, Lady Louisa, born in 1775. She also didn't marry and died in 1875 after spending nearly all her time on her estate. All her life she had carried on a love affair with Traquair House. She looked after the gardens, took great pride in keeping the house itself in perfect order, and, though she was the first female head of the family in many centuries, she had the full respect of the villagers and of her servants. When she died, the question of the inheritance had to be settled by the courts. Eventually, Traquair House passed into the hands of Lady Louisa's cousin, the Honorable Henry Constable Maxwell Stuart, who thus became the sixteenth laird. Perhaps Lady Louisa was not altogether happy with the turn of events, for she had been the last in the direct line to hold Traquair. Possibly, her spirit does not wish to relinquish her realms, or perhaps her long residence here has so accustomed her to Traquair that she is unaware of the fact that there might be another, better place for her to go.

"Has anyone else seen the ghost of Lady Louisa?" I asked the caretaker.

"Well, some other people have seen her, but they have only seen a figure and did not recognize her. Some have seen her farther up the road."

"Why is she called The Green Lady?" I asked. I understood from my friends that the legendary Lady of Traquair was referred to by that name.

"Well, the dress I saw her wearing," the caretaker said, "was kind of green, the color of a wood pigeon."

"Is there such a dress in existence?" I asked. Since so much of the old furniture and personal belongings of the family were preserved at the house, perhaps the original dress still existed.

"Well, it is a strange thing: one of the old foresters here—his wife's mother was Lady Louisa's dressmaker. They kept some of the clippings from which the dresses were made, and when I asked her, the granddaughter showed me the materials. I recognized the color and the material of the dress the lady had on when I saw her." Mr. Burns, the caretaker, admitted that he had some psychic abilities. Sometimes he knew things before they actually occurred, but paid it no great heed.

I asked Mr. Burns to take us to Lady Louisa's room. There, beautifully framed on the south wall, was the great lady's portrait. "She was friendly with Sir Walter Scott," the caretaker commented. The room was oblong, with a fireplace on one end. Wine-red chairs, two sofas, and a strange mixture of eighteenth-century and Victorian furniture gave the room a warm, intimate feeling. On one side, one could gaze into the garden, while the other overlooked the driveway, so that Lady Louisa would always know who was coming up to see her. Alanna hadn't said anything for quite a while. I found her standing by the garden windows. The rain had stopped, and the sun began to pierce through the clouds.

"Do you feel her presence?" I asked.

Alanna gave me a curious look. "Don't you?"

I nodded. I had known for several minutes that Lady Louisa Stuart was at home this afternoon, receiving *unexpected* visitors.

Shortly afterwards, we drove back towards Edinburgh. We crossed the river Tweed again, and the rain started up once more. It was as if fate had held it back for an hour or so to give us a chance to visit Traquair House at its best.

I wondered what it was that bound all British ghosts together. Then it struck me: whether Medieval or Victorian, Renaissance or Edwardian, they all had *style*.